Buddhism

Bud...

for AS students

by Wendy Dossett

Series Editor: Roger J Owen

Acknowledgements

Conversations with a number of people have helped to shape the contents of this book. The author would like to thank: *Patch Cockburn, Catherine, Man Yao, Surana, and friends at the Cardiff Buddhist Centre.*

Credits

Andy Weber: front cover, p. 23, 25(r), 37, 42, 43, 44, 45, 47, 49, 69, 71(c); Amaravati Buddhist Monastery, Hertfordshire: p. 6, 28, 57; photo© Dolf Hartsuiker, from his book Sadhus: Holy Men of India, published by Thames and Hudson Ltd., London:
p. 7; CIBY, France/Simkins Partnership/Recorded Picture Company: p. 11; from the Añguttara-Nikaya, I: 145-6, in F.L. Woodward, Gradual Sayings, Pali Text Society, 1932 Vol. 1, pp. 128-9: p. 11; World Religions/Christine Osborne Pictures: t. 12, 21(c), 56, 59, 63, 71(b), 72; with thanks to The London Buddhist Vihara: p. 13; reproduced by permission of Penguin Books Ltd: p. 14-15, 41; Clear Vision Trust: p. 16; from World Religions: Eastern Traditions, edited by Willard G. Oxtoby (Toronto: Oxford University Press Canada 1996). Copyright © Willard G. Oxtoby 1996. Reprinted by permission of Oxford University Press Canada: p. 20; Tegwyn Roberts: p. 32; Barbara Connell: p. 34; Sussex Academic Press: p. 35; The Foundations of Buddhism (p. 429), Rupert Gethin, 1998. Reprinted by permission of Oxford University Press: p. 37; reprinted by permission of the publisher from Buddhism in Translations: Passages Selected from the Buddhist Sacred Books and translated from the original Pali into English by Henry Clarke Warren, Student's Edition, Harvard Oriental Series. 3., pp. 289-9, Cambridge, Mass.: Harvard University Press, Copyright © 1953 by the President and Fellows of Harvard College: p. 38; by courtesy of the Zenrin-ji Temple, Kyoto/Kyoto National Museum: p. 52; Sile: p. 54; Peter Harvey, An Introduction to Buddhism: Teachings, History and Practices, 1990, Cambridge University Press: p. 68; Arvid Parry Jones: p. 70.
All other photographs are the author's.

Roger J. Owen, Series Editor

Roger J. Owen was Head of RE in a variety of schools for thirty years, as well as being a Head of Faculty, advisory teacher for primary and secondary RE, Section 23 Inspector and 'O' Level and GCSE Chief Examiner. Author of seventeen educational titles, he is currently an education consultant and WJEC Religious Studies AS and A2 Chair of Examiners.

Published by UWIC Press
UWIC, Cyncoed Road,
Cardiff CF23 6XD
cgrove@uwic.ac.uk
029 2041 6515

ISBN 1-902724-58-5

Design by *the info group*
Picture research by *Gwenda Lloyd Wallace*
Printed by *HSW Print*

Commissioned with the financial assistance of Awdurdod Cymwysterau, Cwricwlwm ac Asesu Cymru / the Qualifications, Curriculum and Assessment Authority for Wales (ACCAC).

Buddhism
for AS students
by Wendy Dossett
Series Editor: Roger J Owen

Contents

Buddhism

Introduction

This book is written primarily for students studying AS level Buddhism in Wales. Commissioned by ACCAC, it takes account of the Curriculum Cymreig, otherwise stated as the need for pupils to be "given opportunities, where appropriate, to develop and apply their knowledge and understanding of the cultural, economic, environmental, historical and linguistic characteristics of Wales." As such many of its references and examples have a Welsh flavour. This is an appropriate emphasis in a book which has been commissioned, written, and marketed in a Welsh context. It does not mean the book cannot be used in England or elsewhere.

The book assumes no prior knowledge about Buddhism, and presents the religion in such a way as to meet the requirements of the WJEC AS specification. However, under no circumstances should this book be used as the sole textbook for the Buddhism course, since advanced study requires the skills of wide reading and the analysis of a range of scholarly views on different issues.

The book is designed to be used in tandem with the teachers' book, which provides more detailed background information on some of the topics covered and assistance with the tasks that appear in the text.

AS level candidates are expected to demonstrate not only knowledge and understanding, but also certain skills, such as the ability to sustain a critical line of argument, to justify a point of view, and to relate elements of their course of study to their broader context, as well as to specified aspects of human experience. Some of the tasks that appear below are designed to assist in developing those skills. Teachers and students will doubtless think of others. It is important to remember at all times, however, to go beyond the simple facts about Buddhism, which are relatively easy to learn, and to respond to all aspects of the religion in an open, empathetic and critically aware manner. Being able to appreciate different points of view is crucial in this regard.

This book, and the accompanying teachers' book, is constructed with Key Skills in mind. Students are asked to develop communication skills by taking part in discussions, gathering information and writing. They are asked to develop ICT skills through encouragement to make critically aware use of the Internet, and to present findings in the form of project dossiers and class presentations. They are asked to solve problems through making cases for particular viewpoints, and to work with others on joint research projects. They are also asked to reflect on their own learning and performance by using the self-assessment sheets provided in the teachers' book.

The students' and teachers' books both attempt to reflect the diversity of Buddhism. Not only is this a requirement of the WJEC AS Specification, but it is also crucial to a proper, rounded understanding of the religion. All religious traditions contain a range of viewpoints and practices and students should be able to demonstrate a critical yet non-judgmental awareness of this fact. Teachers and students should take every opportunity to show the diversity of Buddhism. To do otherwise is to risk a partial view of the religion, which could lead to unhelpful stereotyping.

As well as demonstrating awareness of the diversity of Buddhism as a religion, students should also be able to demonstrate awareness that scholarly views of aspects of Buddhism are diverse too. No one writer's view of a religion could be described as objective. Each writer brings to the study of Buddhism their own unique view, including the writer of this text-book. Students should therefore be seeking to present the views of a number of writers. These views need not be classic arguments or philosophical positions, merely the way in which a writer presents certain aspects of the religion.

Note about the Languages

When studying Buddhism, students will encounter words from a number of different languages. This is sometimes a little confusing. It is important however for students to learn these terms because, for every term learnt, something important about Buddhism is also learnt.

Sometimes different spellings of the same term will be encountered. This is because some of the languages involved are different but similar. There is a general rule that Pali terms are used when the context is Theravada Buddhism, and Sanskrit terms are used when the context is Mahayana Buddhism (unless, of course, it is specifically Japanese Buddhism or Tibetan Buddhism or the Buddhism of another country being spoken about). However, there are lots of times when Buddhism is being spoken about in its widest sense, and then either spelling is used.

In this book:
(P)   = Pali (the ancient language of the Theravada scriptures).
(Skt)   = Sanskrit (the ancient holy language of India, in which the Hindu scriptures
           are written, and in which many of the Mahayana scriptures are written).
(Jap)   = Japanese
(Tib)   = Tibetan

Note about the Dates

This book uses the abbreviations CE and BCE for Common Era and Before the Common Era. Some books use AD (Anno Domini) for CE and BC (Before Christ) for BCE. The actual years are the same, only the tag is different.

The Life of the Buddha

Aim of the Section

This section will ask you to consider not only the details of the life of the historical Buddha, but also his role and significance in Buddhism.

This means that you will need to consider five key issues:

1 **The historical background and context for both the life and the teachings of the Buddha.**

2 **The relationship between the teachings of the Buddha and the other beliefs of his time.**

3 **The meaning of elements in the biography of the Buddha for Buddhists today.**

4 **The different ways in which the Buddha is understood in different traditions of Buddhism.**

5 **The relationship between the concepts of 'Buddha' and 'Buddhahood' and the idea of the bodhisattva.**

India at the Time of the Buddha

Aim

After studying this chapter you should be able to demonstrate clear knowledge and understanding of the beliefs about self, reincarnation, caste, duty, and renunciation that were dominant beliefs at the time of the Buddha. These are important ideas, partly because the Buddha both used and criticised them in his own teachings, and partly because they provide the context for his life story. You should also be able to explain your responses to these beliefs, by using critical argument and justifications for your point of view.

The man who was to become the Buddha was born in ancient Northern India, or modern day Nepal. Some 2,500 years ago, at the time of the Buddha, the religion of the people who lived there was later to develop into modern Hinduism. Whilst the general religious scene at the the time was one of a number of competing teachers and doctrines, each with different understandings of the world, a number of important ideas were begining to emerge.

The Soul

The idea that every individual had an eternal, unchanging soul was a central belief of the time. The earliest Sanskrit texts used by the priests and scholars, the Vedas, spoke of the soul as the 'breath' of the divine, but by the time of the Buddha the idea was becoming more developed. The texts known as the Upanishads, some of which are usually dated a little later than the life of the Buddha, though of course they drew on ideas that believers had discussed for centuries, described the idea of the soul in much more depth. In the Upanishads, the soul (in Sanskrit 'atman') is said to be found in all living beings, not only humans and it is described as being 'identical' with Brahman, or the divine. In other words, not only does every being have an eternal soul, but that eternal soul IS God. A famous phrase in the Upanishads, Tat Tvam Asi – 'that thou art' or 'you are that', sums up this idea that, at heart, all beings are divine.

Seminar topic

How does this definition of the soul compare to ideas to be found in other religions?

For reflection

Do you believe that all beings have a soul? How would you explain or justify your answer to someone who did not share your view?

Reincarnation

The soul of each being is eternal and unchanging and can be reborn into different human or animal existences. When the body dies, the soul lives on, and transmigrates to another existence. This is reincarnation. 'Incarnation' means 'in the flesh', and the 're-' part of the word indicates that it happens again and again. In fact, at the time of the Buddha most people believed that their atman (soul) had had thousands of previous lives. The force that drives this reincarnation was known as karma, or 'action'. Karma is the principle of cause and effect and has a moral quality to it. This means that if you do something good there is a good effect, and if you do something bad there is a bad effect. In ancient Indian thought, a person's situation in life was thought to be the 'fruit' or result of their karma. This belief that positive action has a positive effect, meant that it was possible, with effort, to 'purify' your karma and make it good. This would lead the atman eventually to moksha, liberation of the atman from the endless round of reincarnation to be united with God. Moksha was the religious goal of people at the time of the Buddha.

Seminar topic

Is it reasonable to believe in reincarnation? If so, why? If not, why not?

The class and caste system

Like most societies in the world, the society of ancient India was hierarchical: however in India this was expressed in religious terms. Some groups were considered more ritually pure than others. Ritual purity has nothing to do with actual cleanliness; it is rather a symbolic state associated with elite groups. The ritual purity of a person can be damaged by contact with anyone from a less ritually pure group, so such people are best avoided.

In India at the time of the Buddha there were four main groups or classes (varnas), and these were each subdivided into numerous occupational groups or castes (jatis). A person belonged to their class and caste as a result of their birth, which was understood as simply the fruition of karma from past lives, and they stayed in that class and caste all their life. They would be unable to mix with, eat with, or form relationships with people in classes lower than their own, because they would be thought of as ritually impure.

The main classes or varnas were

The Brahmins	or the priests and scholars. At the time of the Buddha, these people were very powerful, because only they could perform the rituals needed to keep the gods on good terms with the community.
The Kshatriyas	the rulers and warriors (India was not a unified country, and there were many regions, administrated by local rulers).
The Vaishyas	the merchants and farmers.
The Shudras	the workers and servants.

In addition to these classes there was another group emerging, later to be known as the Untouchables or the Dalits. It is now illegal in India to discriminate on the basis of class or caste, but at the time of the Buddha, the Untouchables would have been considered extremely ritually impure. They would have jobs like butchery, leatherwork and cremation (i.e. associated with death, which itself is thought of as ritually impure).

Duty

It was believed at the time that the universe was ordered. Each person had a role to play within it, and if they fulfilled that role the universe would operate harmoniously. If they stepped outside of their given role, then they threatened the cosmic order. Their role was their duties, or dharma, the nature of which would be determined by their class (varna), and by their 'stage of life' (ashrama). For example, it would be the duty of a Kshatriya man to learn the skills required to be a leader of people, to rule them justly and to defend them if necessary. When the time was right it would be his duty to marry a Kshatriya woman, to have children, and to bring his sons up to follow in his footsteps (i.e. to help them fulfil their dharma as Kshatriyas).

Evaluate the view that harmony depends on everybody doing the tasks alloted to them.

Seminar topic

Is the class and caste system fair? Is the ancient Indian system different from the class system in Britain? What is it that defines the classes in Britain and India? For instance, is it education, income, tradition? Justify your views.

Renunciation

The tradition of breaking ties with family and community, giving up possessions, the comfort of a home, sexual relationships, a bed to sleep on, any food additional to what is required merely to survive, and 'going forth' on a spiritual quest, was a fairly common feature of life in ancient India. However, it was a step usually taken towards the end of life, after all other duties (such as having a family and a job) had been fulfilled. In this case the person was known as a Sannyasin. Occasionally, someone would decide to go forth early in life, before other duties had been performed. At the time of the Buddha such a person was called a sramana. In modern Hinduism they are called sadhus. Renouncing early in life is not orthodox (religiously correct practice), because it breaks with conventional dharma.

The reason why such extreme practices were performed was the belief that it was the needs and desires of the physical body that prevented the soul's liberation. On page 1 is a discussion of the belief that the atman is Brahman. This was believed to be the case, but it was thought to be very difficult to actually realise it in practice. To truly know this would be more than just an intellectual thing, it would be a deep experience, and of course it would probably take lifetimes of effort to achieve it.

Since the needs and desires of the physical body were seen as the obstacle to this understanding of the self, they needed to be firmly controlled. Therefore the mind and body would be trained to cope with pain, and to be indifferent to both pleasure and suffering. Some renunciates (ascetics) performed extraordinary feats, such as spending years standing on one leg or holding an arm in the air, in order to train themselves to overcome physical pain, in the belief that if reactions to the body were controlled, the soul could be liberated. Others made somewhat less extreme sacrifices, but the aim was the same: to avoid the distractions of worldly life and to direct the soul towards liberation.

A modern Indian ascetic performing austerities. This man has held his arm up for twelve years.

What are the benefits of training the body to cope with pain?

Seminar topic

Many religions ask their followers to renounce things for spiritual reasons (e.g. fasting in Ramadan, or giving something up during Lent). Why do you think this is?

Tasks

Research task	Using the internet and other sources, discover examples of the practices of modern day sadhus. The festival of the Kumbh Mela in 2001 saw many thousands of sadhus perform their practices (known as austerities) in the same place. Try to explain their intentions.
Writing task	Explain the importance of the belief in atman to ancient Indians at the time of the Buddha.

Glossary

atman	The eternal soul. A concept widely believed in at the time of the Buddha (but not by him), and now a feature of most types of Hinduism.
Brahman	God in the religion of India at the time of the Buddha. Sometimes Brahman would be described as the 'universal soul' and some people believed that atman and Brahman were essentially the same.
brahmins	The highest varna. Priests and scholars, and the most ritually pure.
Dalits	Literally 'the opressed'. Untouchables, considered extremely ritually impure.
dharma	'law', 'duty', obligation'. Traditionally Indians believed that there was a universal law, or cosmic order, and each individual must play their role in this by performing their own appropriate duties.
jati	Occupational group.
karma	'action'. People at the time of the Buddha believed that it was karma that determined the transmigration of the atman. Buddhists understand karma as resulting from the person's 'intentions'. It is karma that shapes personality.
kshatriyas	The second highest varna. Warriors and rulers. The Buddha was born into the kshatriya varna.
Kumbh Mela	A festival that happens in India every twelve years, at which sadhus gather together to bathe in the Ganges and to perform austerities.
ritual purity	This is the idea that some people are more pure than others. The person's purity can be changed by the way they behave, or by people or objects with which they come into contact. For example the ritual purity of a Brahmin would be changed if he encountered a dead body, or if he had an affair, or if he ate food prepared by a dalit. Sometimes ritual purity is demonstrated by symbolic washing. For example, a statue of a god may be washed to show that it is ritually pure. Indians would wash before performing puja (worship).
sadhu	An ascetic in the Hindu tradition. Someone who has given up family and communit life, and who performs austerities, as part of the quest for the liberation of the soul.
sannyasin	Someone who gives up community and family towards the end of life, in order to prepare for death.
Sanskrit	The ancient language of India in which the Hindu scriptures are written. Many Mahayana Buddhist scriptures are also written in Sanskrit.
shudras	The lowest varna. The labourers.
sramana	An ascetic from the time of the Buddha.
tat tvam asi	'You are that' or 'That thou art'. A phrase that comes up again and again in the Upanishads, that refers to the idea that the atman is divine.
Upanishads	Important Hindu scriptures that explain beliefs about atman and Brahman.
vaishyas	The third varna. The farmers and merchants.
varna	Literally 'colour'. The groupings of people according to ritual purity, in the ancient four level hierarchy.
Vedas	The main body of Hindu scriptures. The Buddha rejected the authority of the Vedas in favour of the authority of experience.

Key Events in the Life of the Buddha

Aim

After studying this chapter you should be able to demonstrate clear knowledge and understanding of the key events in the life of the historical Buddha. You should have some critical awareness of the issue of historical accuracy, and you should be able to show that you understand how Buddhists find inspiration in the story. You should also be able to demonstrate your own responses to the story.

As we have seen, the man who became known as the Buddha was born centuries before the beginning of the Common Era. Nothing was written down about his life until centuries after he had died. Accounts of his life were remembered by his followers, who repeated them in order to memorise them. By the time the story of his life was committed to writing, the Sangha (Buddhist Community) had decided what they thought Buddhists ought to know about this man.

Did he really exist?

The scholar Michael Pye writes 'It is simply not possible to explain the origin of early Buddhism in a sensible way unless a creative leader such as the Buddha is presumed to have lived. This argument does not prove the reality of any of the particular details in his history, but it does enable us to point with some confidence to the time, the place and the character of his activity.'[1]

For many Buddhists the life-story of the Buddha is very important. However, some Buddhists say that even if the Buddha had not existed, or even if someone else had found the way to enlightenment, it wouldn't make any difference to Buddhism. He merely found a way that was always there and could have been found by anyone. Buddhists believe that it has been found by others and is still being found by some today.

> **Seminar topic**
>
> *Which is more important, the Buddha or his teaching?*

How many Buddhas?

Buddhists believe that there are many existences other than this one we have in our human 'realm' in our historical period. There are many other realms, and many other ages. Therefore there are many other Buddhas. The man whom we refer to in this book as 'the Buddha' is often given the title 'the historical Buddha' by scholars to show that he is the Buddha of our realm and time period, and to indicate that he is one amongst many others. For example, other Buddhas feature in the accounts of the previous lives of the historical Buddha - the Jataka Tales, and other Buddhas are venerated or honoured in the many different traditions of Buddhism.

A man or a god?

Different traditions of Buddhism describe the Buddha in different ways. In Theravada Buddhism, the type to be found in countries such as Sri Lanka and Thailand, the Buddha is seen very much as a human being and as an example to others on the quest for enlightenment. Buddhists in general do not consider the Buddha to be a god. Hindus believe that God comes to earth in the form of avatars or 'manifestations', but Buddhists do not believe that the Buddha was an avatar either. There are stories in the Buddha's biography about supernatural events that in other religious traditions would be associated with gods. These stories demonstrate the importance of the Buddha, and indicate the value that those who wrote about him put on his achievement. The appearance of a Buddha in the world is special, and the writers of his biography show this by recording some of the events that had special meaning for the followers of the Buddha at that time. Buddhists are not asked to believe the whole story word for word. It is a story that comes from a different time. However, it does help to illustrate many of the key ideas in Buddhism, and Buddhists use it for inspiration, to help them practice their religion.

There are many different sources for the traditional account of the life of the Buddha, and no authorised version. There is no one book that contains the whole story, although the book most frequently referred to is Ashvaghosha's Buddhacarita (The Acts of the Buddha). This is a first century text, so written hundreds of years after the death of the Buddha. Certain key events feature in many of the scriptural accounts of the Buddha and have become very important to the traditional life-story often told by Buddhists. These events are his birth; the four sights or signs; his renunciation or 'going forth'; his enlightenment; his decision to teach; and his death.

The names of the Buddha.

Before he becomes enlightened at the age of 35, the Buddha is usually known by his given name of *Siddattha* (P) or *Siddhartha* (S). You will find both spellings in the books you read, because the life story of the Buddha comes from two languages, *Sanskrit* (S) and *Pali* (P). You may also find him referred to as *Gotama* (P) or *Gautama* (S). Sometimes he is given the title *'The Bodhisattva'*, which in this case means *'The Buddha-to-be'*. After his enlightenment, he is known by his title *'The Buddha'* which means *'The Enlightened One'*. Other names include *Shakyamuni*, which means *'Sage of the Shakya Clan'*.

His birth and upbringing

Scholars debate the date of the birth of Siddhartha. It is often given as 563BCE, but recently this date has been thrown into doubt by historians who argue that it could not have been earlier than 411BCE. Tradition states that Siddhartha was born in the Lumbini Grove in Northern India in what is present-day Nepal. His parents, Suddhodana and Maya, were Kshatriyas (see page 2) and his father was the local ruler.

Seminar topic

Many Buddhists emphasise the humanity of the Buddha. Some of the stories about his conception and birth seem out of keeping with this emphasis. How might these stories be explained?

The accounts of his conception and birth contain miraculous stories. These are very interesting because they help to show the significance of the birth of Siddhartha. Maya dreamt of an elephant entering her womb (elephants are auspicious [lucky] creatures), before discovering she was pregnant. When the time came, she gave birth through her side whilst leaning against a tree. In some traditions of Indian thought anything to do with sex and childbirth is thought to be polluting. These stories show that Siddhartha is supposed to be thought of as pure, different and special. As soon as he was born, the story goes, he walked seven steps and announced 'I was born for enlightenment, and for the good of all that lives. This is my last birth into this world'.

At Siddhartha's naming ceremony, a famous seer called Asita prophesied that Siddhartha would become either a great leader of his people, or a great holy man. This disturbed Suddhodana greatly because, as a Kshatriya, Siddhartha would be expected to follow in his father's footsteps. The scriptures say that Suddhodana took steps to ensure that Siddhartha was not exposed to any influence that might encourage him to reflect on the meaning of life in a religious way. The boy was effectively imprisoned in paradise. He had all his needs and wants met. He was shielded from the sadder side of life that we experience as we grow up. He was surrounded by young, beautiful, healthy people. He never saw anything die, not even an animal or a plant. He grew into a hearty young man, good at sports and skilled in arts, mathematics and indeed anything he turned his hand to. He married the beautiful princess Yasodhara. In fact he seemed to be fulfilling the prophecy made by Asita that he would become a great leader of his people – until, that is, the time of the birth of his son, who was named Rahula (meaning 'fetters' or 'chains'). Siddhartha was 29 years old, and he was restless. Perhaps the name he gave to his son was an indication of his psychological state at this time.

Siddhartha (played by Keanu Reeves in the film 'The Little Buddha') meditating under the Bodhi tree.

The Buddha describes the life in his father's palace.

Monks, I was delicately nurtured, exceeding delicately nurtured, delicately nurtured beyond measure. For instance in my father's house lotus-pools were made thus: one of blue lotuses, one of red, another of white lotuses, just for my benefit. No sandalwood powder did I use that was not the best: of the best cloth was my turban made: of the best cloth was my jacket, my tunic and my cloak. By night and day a white canopy was held over me, lest cold or heat or dust or chaff or dew should touch me. Moreover, monks, I had three palaces: one for winter, one for summer and one for the rainy season. In the four months of the rains I was waited on by minstrels, women all of them. Whereas in other men's homes broken rice together with sour gruel is given as food to slave servants, in my father's home they were given rice, meat and milk-rice for their food.

From the Anguttara Nikaya; translation adapted from Whitfield Foy's, Man's Religious Quest, Open University Press, 1978

The Four Sights

Siddhartha decided that he could no longer go on without knowing about the world outside. He made four fateful journeys to the outside world, where he was to witness four sights that changed his life completely. Buddhists see these four sights as crucial to understanding what Buddhism is about.

On the first journey he saw an old man. Age was a completely new concept to Siddhartha, and he realised for the first time that those he loved, and he himself would become old. On the second journey he saw a diseased man, and his charioteer, Channa, who accompanied him, told him that most people experience sickness in their lives. This was a second shock for Siddhartha. It could not, however, prepare him for his third devastating experience, which was the sight of a funeral procession with a corpse. Siddhartha had, up until that point, known nothing of death. He had not realised that life was finite; that his wife, his son, his father, himself, and every living thing would inevitably die. This new knowledge affected him so deeply that he wept with compassion for all beings. He could not return to his life of pleasure, because those pleasures had become tainted by his knowledge that they would pass and be replaced by sickness, old age and death.

On his fourth journey he saw a wandering Hindu sramana or sadhu (ascetic). Though the man was old and without possessions, his faced appeared serene and peaceful. This inspired Siddhartha. Obviously, the sadhu knew about sickness, old age and death; and yet he was not in the state of total despair that Siddhartha was currently experiencing. He must know the secret, the answer to the question of the meaning of life. Siddhartha resolved to follow the same path.

For reflection

Can you remember at what points in your life you became aware of the suffering and mortality? How did it feel?

The iconography of the period of Siddhartha's austerities shows the extreme lengths to which he went to attain liberation.

Siddhartha compared this period to his life of luxury in the palace. Why was this?

His Renunciation

Renouncing or giving up family life in order to search for spiritual truth was a common practice in India, but Siddhartha's renunciation was precisely the event that Suddhodana had been trying to avoid. After all, he was a Kshatriya, with responsibilities to his family and to his tribe. However, Siddhartha was intent on finding an answer to the question of why we suffer, and how we can transcend or overcome it. He left his wife and new-born son, gave up his fabulous life at the palace, shaved his head, and gave his horse to Channa, his faithful charioteer.

He then 'went forth' and embarked on the Hindu path to liberation (see page 3). He had a number of teachers, and practiced austerities with a group of five other ascetics. For six years he attempted to suppress his bodily needs and desires in order to liberate his soul. He limited his intake of food and became so thin that he could touch his spine by pressing on his stomach. Eventually he realised that he would kill himself if he persisted, and that he was no less despairing than when he had started. He bathed and ate some gruel. At this, his five disappointed companions left him in disgust.

However, Siddhartha was still intent on his quest. He declared that the truth was not to be found through a life of extremes – either of luxury or of renunciation. The best way was the Middle Way. He sat down beneath a Banyan tree, vowing to remain there until he had achieved what he had set out to do. As he meditated through the night the demon Mara attempted to frighten him from his quest and undermine his confidence, and Mara's beautiful daughters (named 'Thirst', 'Passion' and 'Desire') were instructed to attempt to seduce him. All attempts to distract Siddhartha failed and, as dawn approached, he attained enlightenment.

For reflection

Is it possible to be rich and religious at the same time?

His Enlightenment

Buddhists argue that the attainment or achievement that earned Siddhartha the title of 'the Buddha' ('the Enlightened One') cannot be described in words. It is a state or experience that is beyond everything we know. Our words could not capture its meaning. Only an enlightened person can understand it. The Buddhist fable of the turtle and the fish illustrates the impossibility of describing something outside of our experience, and the foolishness of dismissing the possibility of things we cannot test.

Reading The Turtle and the Fish

Once upon a time there lived a fish and a turtle who were friends. The fish, having lived all his life in the water, knew nothing whatever about anything else. One day, as the fish was swimming in the water, he met his friend, the turtle, who had just returned from an excursion on land. On being told this, the fish said, 'On dry land! What do you mean by 'dry land'? I have never seen such a thing – 'dry land' is nothing!' 'Well', said the turtle, 'you are at liberty to think so, but that is where I've been all the same.' 'Oh, come on,' said the fish, 'try to talk sense. Just tell me, what is this 'land' of yours like? Is it all wet?'
'No, it is not wet,' said the turtle.
'Is it nicely fresh and cool?' asked the fish.
'No, it is not fresh and cool,' replied the turtle.
'Is it clear so that light can come through it?'
'No, it is not clear. Light cannot come through it.'
'Is it soft and yielding so that I can move my fins about in it and push my nose through it.'
'No, it is not soft and yielding. You cannot swim in it.'
'Does it move or flow in streams? Does it ever rise up into waves with white foam on them?' asked the fish, becoming rather impatient at the string of No's.
'No,' replied the turtle, 'it never rises up into waves.'
The fish then asked, 'If the land is not a single one of these things, what else is it but nothing?'
'Well,' said the turtle, 'if you are determined to think that 'dry land' is nothing, I cannot help you. But anyone who knows what is water and what is land would say you were a silly fish, for you think that anything you have never known is nothing, just because you have never known it.'

Adapted from H Saddhatissa, What is Nibbana?
London British Mahabodhi Society, London, 1984, pp9-11

It is important to remember that anything that is said about enlightenment is provisional and incomplete. That is, it gives us some idea about it, but does not encapsulate the whole meaning of the condition. This is because the words we have at our disposal refer to things in ordinary human experience, not to things that lie outside of it. We are like the fish, who had no conception of, or words for, 'dry land'. Perhaps the best way to try to understand it is to look at what the Buddha said after he had attained it, and the things he taught about for the rest of his life. We shall explore this in more depth later on. It is also helpful to look at what the scriptures say he experienced. The Buddha is said to have become aware of his own past lives and the past lives of all the beings in the universe. He saw that everything is linked by cause and effect, and that everything is constantly changing. He saw that suffering comes from craving and attachment; the belief that things, or people, or ideas can bring us happiness, when in fact they themselves are subject to change, so cannot provide satisfaction. With this realisation he is said to have overcome all craving and attachment himself and experienced the peace of nirvana. Nirvana is a word often used as an alternative to enlightenment, and indicates the ending of all suffering.

The scriptures put it like this:

Reading The Four Watches of the Night

This passage is quite complex, and there are some concepts in it that may be difficult to understand at this stage. However, it gives a sense of the importance and of the impact of what the Buddha had achieved. Look particularly at the last paragraph of the passage. Why would the biographers of the Buddha wish to speak of flowers falling from the skies, and even non-human beings 'great seers among the host of invisible beings' proclaiming his fame?

In the first watch of the night he recollected the successive series of his former births…. When he had recalled his own births and deaths in all these various lives of his, the Sage, full of pity, turned his compassionate mind towards other living beings and he thought to himself: 'Again and again they must leave the people they regard as their own, and must go on elsewhere, and that without ever stopping. Surely this world is unprotected and helpless, and like a wheel it turns round and round'. As he continued steadily to recollect the past thus, he came to the definite conviction that this world of samsara is as insubstantial as the pith of plantain tree.

Second to none in valour he then, in the second watch of the night, acquired the supreme heavenly eye…. He saw that the decease and rebirth of beings depend on whether they have done superior or inferior deeds. And his compassion grew still further. It became clear to him that no security can be found in this flood of samsaric existence, and that they threat of death is ever-present. Beset on all sides, creatures can find no resting place….

Then as the third watch of that night drew on, the supreme master of trance turned his meditation to the real and essential nature of this world: 'Alas, living beings wear themselves out in vain! Over and over again they are born, they age they die, pass on to a new life, and are reborn! What is more, greed and dark delusion obscure their sight, and they are blind from birth.' He then surveyed the twelve links of conditioned co-production, and saw that beginning with ignorance, they lead to old age and death, and, beginning with cessation of ignorance, they lead to cessation of birth, old age, death and all kinds of ill.

When the great seer had comprehended that where there is no ignorance whatever, there also the karma formations are stopped – then he had achieved a correct knowledge of all there is to be known, and he stood out in the world as a Buddha… From the summit of the world downwards he could detect no self anywhere. Like the fire, when its fuel is burnt up, he became tranquil. He had reached perfection, and he thought to himself: 'This is the authentic Way on which in the past so many great seers, who also knew all higher and all lower things, have travelled on to ultimate and real truth. And now I obtained it!'

At that moment, in the fourth watch of the night…. the earth swayed like a woman drunken with wine, the sky shone bright with the siddhas who appeared in crowds in all the directions, and the mighty drums of thunder resounded through the air. Pleasant breezes blew softly, rain fell from a cloudless sky, flowers and fruits dropped from the trees out of season – in an effort to show reverence for him. Mandarava flowers and lotus blossoms, and also water-lilies made of gold and beryl, fell from the sky on to the ground near the Shakya Sage, so that it looked like a place in the world of the gods.

At the moment, no one anywhere was angry, ill, or sad; no one did evil, none was proud; the world became quite quiet, as though it had reached full perfection. Joy spread through the ranks of those gods who longed for salvation; joy also spread among those who lived in the regions below. Everywhere the virtuous were strengthened, the influence of dharma increased, and the world rose from the dirt of the passions and the darkness of ignorance. Filled with joy and wonder at the Sage's work, the seers of the solar race who had been protectors of men, who had been royal seers, who had been great seers, stood in their mansions in the heavens and showed him their reverence. The great seers among the hosts of invisible beings could be heard widely proclaiming his fame.

Adapted from The Buddhacarita by Ashvaghosha trans. in E. Conze Buddhist Scriptures, London, Penguin , 1959 pp48-53

His decision to teach

After his enlightenment, the Buddha was unsure whether he would be able to communicate it, for the reasons mentioned above. However, the story goes that the god Brahma persuaded him that he must share his knowledge, and the Buddha vowed 'Having myself crossed the ocean of suffering, I must help others to cross it. Freed myself, I must set others free'. The first people he taught were the Five Ascetics who had denounced and rejected him him earlier, but who now accepted him as a fully enlightened Buddha. His first sermon is sometimes referred to as The Deer Park Sermon, because of where it took place, or as the 'First Turning of the Wheel of the Dharma' (dharma means the teachings or truths of Buddhism).

For the next forty-five years the Buddha taught about the truths he had realised under the tree (now referred to as the Bodhi Tree - bodhi means enlightenment) to anyone who would listen. He used stories, parables and metaphors to try to help people understand what could not be explained, only experienced. He gained a huge following, including poor people and women, as well as kings and even gods. Those who wished to join the community or Sangha took vows and adopted a strict lifestyle.

Death

The Buddha is said to have died after a bout of food poisoning. He knew that his death was imminent, and continued to receive his followers whilst he lay down between two trees. Ananda, a close disciple of the Buddha, was worried about the future of the community without its teacher, and was upset at the thought of his dear master dying. The Buddha declared that whoever sees the dharma (teachings) sees the Buddha also, implying not only that the teachings themselves were his successor, but that he and the teachings were one. He told Ananda not to weep, since it is in the nature of things to be separated from those who are dear to us. His last words were 'All conditioned things are perishable. Work out your own salvation with diligence – be a lamp unto yourselves.'

The Parnirvana of the Buddha - with Ananda at his head.

Can you understand Ananda's sorrow at the death of his master? Do you think the Buddha's response was heartless?

He let go of life peacefully. The moment of his death is celebrated in iconography all over the Buddhist world. At the time of his death Buddhists say he had no 'karmic attachments' – all his karma had been used up– so he was not reborn.
This moment is known as the parinirvana or Mahaparinirvana – the Great and Final Nirvana of the Buddha.

Sile and David are members of the Cardiff Buddhist Centre. They spoke about what the death of the Buddha means to them at the Parinirvana celebrations at the centre.

Sile	'Death is something we shun in the West, yet its something that we are all subject to. Remembering the death of the Buddha should help us to come to terms with our own mortality. Death is part of life! We are also celebrating his great achievement – the fact that he had achieved total liberation and would not be coming back to suffer again.'
David	'Parinirvana Day is about the passing away of the body of the Buddha. In a sense it captures the whole essence of Buddhism. The notion of impermanence encourages you to confront the idea of your own death, and to live life to the full. This does not mean Hedonism (doing what you like) because this is not living life to the full. Living life to the full means living fully in the moment and being mindful.'

David

Tasks

Writing task	Explain the meaning for contemporary Buddhists of events in the life of the Buddha. 'A story 2,500 years old can have no relevance for today.' Assess the validity of this view.
Writing and presentation task	Write a modern version of Siddhartha's early life. Think of everything that we know about suffering, sickness, old age and death, and of all the many different ways in which we know about it, for example through television, radio, newspapers, advertising hoardings. How would a modern Siddhartha's father protect his son from any of that knowledge? What sort of information would the father need to stop his son encountering? Are there differences between the things Suddhodana had to think of, such as sweeping dead leaves out of his son's sight, and the things a modern Suddhodana may have to consider? You could write your account as a dialogue to be performed in front of your class.
Research task	Find out in more detail what was said to have happened at the parinirvana of the Buddha. Compare the death of the Buddha to the death of any other religious founder.

Chapter 2

Glossary

Ananda	The Buddha's cousin and close disciple. Ananda was present at the death of the Buddha and also recited the teachings of the Buddha at the First Council.
Ascetic	Someone who renounces family and community life to seek the path to liberation.
Asita	The rishi, or 'seer', who prophesied that Siddhartha would become either a great ruler or a great religious leader.
banyan / bodhi tree	The type of tree that the Buddha became enlightened under was a Banyan, which is like a fig tree. After his enlightenment it became known as the bodhi tree. Temples all over the Buddhist world have leaves or cuttings from the descendents of this tree. There is a descendent of the original bodhi tree in Bodh Gaya, and Buddhists often make pilgrimages to see it.
Brahma	The creator god in Hinduism.
Buddhacarita	'The Acts of the Buddha'. One of the biographies of the Buddha, written by Ashvaghosha in the first century.
Channa	Siddhartha's charioteer, who accompanied him when he saw the four sights.
enlightenment	The attainment of the Buddha under the Bodhi tree. Buddhists say that this state defies description. The word nirvana is often used as an alternative term.
Jataka Tales	Stories of the previous lives of Siddhartha.
Mara	A demon who attempted to distract Siddhartha from the quest for enlightenment.
Nirvana	The 'blowing out' of the three fires of greed, hatred and ignorance, and the cessation of dukkha. Nirvana is often defined negatively, because it is beyond all of our unenlightened imaginations and our words cannot capture its meaning. It is not usually thought of as a 'place'. Nor is it merely a 'state of mind'.
Pali	An ancient Indian language, and the language of the scriptures recognised by Theravada Buddhists.
parinirvana / mahaparinirvana	The 'final nirvana' – the death of the Buddha.
Rahula	The name of Siddhartha's son. It means 'Chains' or 'Fetters'.
Sangha	The community of Buddhists, or more strictly the community of Buddhist monks and nuns.
Shakyamuni	'Sage of the Shakya clan'. One of the names often used for the Buddha.
Suddhodana	The Buddha's father.
the middle way	The rejection of extremes of luxury or of asceticism. The idea of the middle way becomes very important in Buddhism and is a philosophical concept as well as a lifestyle.
Yasodhara	Siddhartha's wife.

The Buddha: A Human Example

Aim

In this section you will gain knowledge about the development of Buddhism after the death of the Buddha and you will gain an understanding of the Theravada view of the Buddha, as a human being who uncovered the path and who acts as an example to all those committed to seeking enlightenment.

The spread of Buddhism after the death of the Buddha

After his death the teachings of the Buddha were preserved through oral tradition, as was the custom at a time when few could write the sacred language of Sanskrit. Councils of the Buddha's followers were called from time to time to recite the teachings together and inevitably disagreements arose. Eventually, some four centuries later, these disagreements led to the emergence of two distinct types of Buddhism, now known as Theravada, the Way of the Elders, and Mahayana, the Greater Vehicle. By that time, Buddhism had spread over most of India and other parts of South Asia and had even entered China.

A number of great Indian Dynasties, such as the Mauryan Empire from the time of King Asoka onwards, and the Kusana and Gupta Empires, favoured Buddhism and encouraged it to flourish.

Time line

According to tradition. It is very difficult to prove the historical accuracy of some of this information.

- **The Buddha c. 563-483 BCE**

- **1st Council of the Sangha c. 482 BCE at Rajagriha, at which Ananda recited the teachings, and another monk, Upali, recited the rules for the Sangha.**

- **2nd Council of the Sangha c. 373 BCE at Vaisali, at which a disagreement about the rules for monks handling money was discussed**

- **3rd Council of the Sangha c. 250 BCE at Pataliputra, where the beginnings of the separation of two different 'vehicles' of Buddhism may have occurred.**

- **King Asoka –c.268-232 BCE**

- **Buddhism arrives in Sri Lanka c. 250 BCE**

- **Buddhism arrives in China c. 40CE**

- **Kusana Empire 78CE – 319CE**

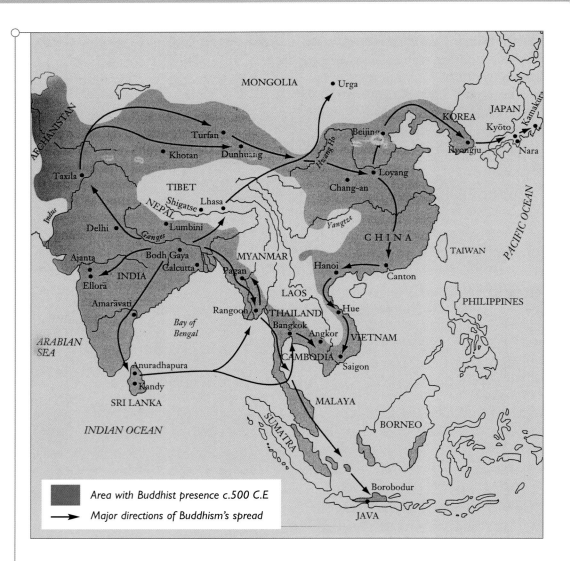

Stupas

Often, once a charismatic teacher has died, his teachings are forgotten. However, the Buddha had always asked his followers not to rely on his authority but to be 'a lamp unto themselves'. They did not have to faithfully accept his teachings; quite the contrary, they had to test them out for themselves, to see if they seemed reasonable, to use them and see if they helped on the path to enlightenment. Authority was effectively passed on to the members of the community themselves (the Sangha); not to a single outstanding follower, or to an elite committee, but to the group as a whole.

Of course, the Sangha tried to preserve the memory of their great teacher. As was customary in India, he was cremated. After the cremation, ashes and pieces of charred bone and teeth were claimed by various groups as relics. They were divided up and enshrined in structures called stupas, which were traditionally funeral mounds built to contain the relics of kings. These became places of pilgrimage and temples were also erected around or near them.

For reflection

What do you think the Buddha would have thought about his relics being treated so reverently

The veneration of stupas became one of the foundations of the religion, since it provided a focus for devotion in the absence of the Buddha himself.

Theravada Buddhism, which is found predominantly in Sri Lanka, Thailand and Burma, attributes a great deal of importance to the figure of the Buddha and the celebration of his great achievement. Despite the supernatural features of his biography, he is considered to have been only an extraordinary human being. Theravada Buddhists do not think of him as a god, nor do they worship him - to do so would be to make a mistake about what Buddhism is all about. It is about cultivating freedom from attachment. If you worship something you are arguably attached to it. As Denise Cush puts it, 'It is vital not to forget that he is one of us'.[2] The fact that he is not a god is important not only because he is not to become an object of attachment, but also because it means he can be a true role model and inspiration for ordinary human beings on the path. If he were a god, then he would be something qualitatively different from us, and his achievements would not be relevant to us. It is precisely the fact that he is human that makes him so important.

The Great Stupa at Sanchi in India, which dates from the time of the third century BCE Emperor Asoka, is an impressive example of a Theravada Stupa.

Why do you think such monuments, many of which originally contained relics, possibly even of the Buddha himself, have become so important in Buddhism?

Sile	Sile is a Buddhist who lives and works in Cardiff. She spoke about her respect for the Buddha and the importance of his humanity just before parinirvana celebrations. 'He was a person just like ourselves, but the difference is, he never gave up. The accounts of his dedication overwhelm me, but at the same time, we can achieve what he achieved.'

Chapter 3

Seminar topic

If Theravada Buddhists think the Buddha was just a man, why do they bow and make offerings before his statue?

For Theravada Buddhists, the historical Buddha is the greatest being ever to have lived, and he is widely celebrated in iconography. In Theravada Buddhism, statues are treated with respect. Buddhists will bow and make offerings in front of them (see chapter 10). However, they are not worshipping the Buddha, nor are they asking for help or praying to him in any way. He no longer exists. Their behaviour towards statues should not be mistaken for worship of a god. It is rather a way of showing their gratitude that he, a human being, found and taught the way to enlightenment, so that all beings could benefit. It is also a way of focusing their efforts to attain what he attained.

In Theravada Buddhism, the Buddha is a 'one off'. It is possible to become enlightened, but it is a very rare thing, and it takes lifetimes of dedication to the following of the path to achieve it. In fact, ordinary Theravada Buddhists think more about purifying their karma and gaining merit, to improve their chances of attaining enlightenment in perhaps many lifetimes to come rather than in this life. The word for an enlightened person is arahant (Skt) or arhat (P). The scriptures celebrate the achievements of the arhats, but their enlightenment - just like the potential enlightenment of anyone else - is wholly dependent on the fact that the Buddha taught the way.

Tasks

Research task	Find out what happened after the death of other great religious founders. How did each religion preserve its authority? Did the founder tell his followers that they should consult a book of revelation, a book containing his own writings, or the writings of others? Did he establish a successor of any kind? In what way is the case of the Buddha similar or different?
Writing task	Explain the attitude of Theravada Buddhists to the Buddha.

Glossary

arahant (skt) arhat (p)	Someone who has become enlightened in the Theravada tradition. It literally means 'worthy'.
Asoka	Emperor who converted to Buddhism in the 3rd century BCE and did much to spread Buddhism in India.
Mahayana	'The Greater Vehicle'. One of the two main types of Buddhism. It is found in East and North Asia, as well as in other parts of the world.
Pataliputra	Site of the third Council of the Sangha.
Rajagriha	Site of the first Council of the Sangha.
stupa	A reliquary. A dome shaped container for the remains of the Buddha or other enlightened person. Stupas became centres of pilgrimage and objects of veneration.
Theravada	'The Way of the Elders'. One of the two main types of Buddhism. It is found in Sri Lanka, Burma and Thailand, as well as in other parts of the world.
Vaisali	Site of the second Council of the Sangha.

The Buddha: A Celestial Being

Aim

In this chapter you will gain knowledge and understanding of Mahayanist views about the nature of the Buddha, as merely one among a number of other enlightened beings, or as an instance of the principle of enlightenment. You will explore the notion of Buddhahood. You will also be asked to critically analyse the differences between the Theravada and Mahayana views of the Buddha.

'The Five Dhyani Buddhas'. Dhyani means meditation. These five Buddhas represent different aspects of enlightenment, and Buddhists who follow Tibetan traditions meditate on their qualities. They are Amitbha, Amoghasiddhi, Aksobhya, Ratnasambhava and Vairocana.

Mahayana Buddhism

For both Theravada and Mahayana Buddhists, the teachings are crucial. However, Mahayana Buddhists are less concerned than the Theravada about what the Buddha may or may not have said. They are more concerned with the whole notion of enlightenment itself. The founding philosophers of the Mahayana tradition developed some of the Buddha's key teachings. Since these philosophers were considered to be enlightened themselves, Mahayana Buddhists respect their teachings as much as they do the teachings of the historical Buddha. Whilst Theravada Buddhists see the Buddha as a 'one off', Mahayana Buddhists recognise the potential of all beings to become enlightened Buddhas.

Buddha-nature

The Mahayana Philosophers, for example the 1st century monk, Nagarjuna, focussed on the Buddha's teaching about pratitya samutpada (see chapter 6). This teaching or doctrine tells us that everything is connected. There are no boundaries between ourselves and others, or ourselves and the environment. The unenlightened person sees separateness, but the enlightened person sees only connectedness. Connectedness is the foundation of everything, it is ultimate truth. Nagarjuna reflected that if this was the case, then nirvana and samsara (our unenlightened realm) must be connected too. Nirvana must be not a far off goal, but in a sense present in the here and now. Therefore, the historical Buddha cannot be seen as a one off. Nirvana, or 'Buddha-hood', is equally available to all of us. In fact, all beings must have what is known as the Buddha-nature. Everybody is actually enlightened. The task is to uncover it, or to realise it. This, of course, is not easy!

This philosophy of connectedness influenced the development of Mahayana Buddhism a great deal. As well as the possibility of enlightenment for all beings (even in this life, according to some forms of Mahayana Buddhism), there is also the possibility of encountering enlightened beings other than the Buddha himself.

The Bodhisattvas

In the Mahayana tradition many Buddhists commit themselves to what is known as the Bodhisattva path. Bodhisattva is a Sanskrit word meaning 'Enlightenment Being' (effectively the same meaning as 'Buddha' – Enlightened One). This path involves the progress through stages towards enlightenment, similar to, though slightly different from, the progress made by the person working towards to arhatship. Through practicing the path, the individual gains in wisdom.

This wisdom involves seeing things for what they really are, or realising ultimate truth. What is ultimate truth? According to Mahayana Buddhism, it is that everything is connected. The wise bodhisattva realises this means not only intellectually, but also experientially. As a result they become fully awakened to the sufferings of others, and act spontaneously to help them. So in Mahayana Buddhism there are two important and completely interrelated concepts: wisdom and compassion. These are the qualities shown by the bodhisattva. Mahayana Buddhists believe that bodhisattvas are available to help them on their journey towards enlightenment.

In Buddhism, time and space are thought of as infinite. The Buddha never spoke about creation or the end of the world, nor did he say that the human realm was the only dimension. Mahayana scriptures speak of realms other than this one, and times other than our present historical period, each of which has its own bodhisattva or Buddha. Sometimes these beings are described as 'Celestial Buddhas'. This should not be taken to mean that they are in the sky or in heaven. It really means they have existences other than the human one, though, of course, they may have had a human birth at one time.

Some examples of Buddhas and Bodhisattvas

Avalokitesvara (below left) is one of the most popular of the celestial bodhisattvas. His name means 'He who hears the cries of the world.' In one Tibetan myth, the female enlightened being Tara was born from a tear he shed as he became enlightened (i.e. as he became fully aware of all the sufferings of others).

Manjusri (above right) is depicted with a flaming sword that cuts through ignorance.

Amida (Jap.) (Amitabha, Skt.) (right) is a Buddha who way back in the unimaginable past made a vow out of great compassion to bring all beings to enlightenment (i.e. to bring all beings out of suffering). He vowed to ensure their rebirth in the Pure Land (a realm different from the human realm) where enlightenment would be instant.

Seminar topic

How would you define wisdom?

Surely Theravada Buddhists are right to focus on what the Buddha actually said. Mahayana Buddhists have made up their own form of the religion. That can't be right, can it?

Catherine, a Buddhist who lives in Manchester, explains why one of the five Dhyani Buddhas is important to her.

"Amoghasiddhi is the archetypal Buddha, associated with the northerly direction, the colour deep green and the quality of fearlessness. As such he appeals to me, a white British Buddhist, more attuned to the landscape, climate and myths of northern Europe than to the culture and landscape of Asia. At the moment I simply keep him in mind, but when I am ordained into the Western Buddhist Order, I'll probably choose to take up a meditation practice in which I visualise him and try to bring his qualities to mind, to become more like him myself.

His symbol is a vishva-vajra, or double vajra. The single vajra is a diamond thunderbolt, that symbolises what it would be like suddenly to be struck by ultimate Reality; how it would feel suddenly to see that life as we know it really is impermanent (anicca), and insubstantial (anatta) and unsatisfactory (dukkha). One would be quite simply thunderstruck. The double vajra represents this Reality a thousand times over. It's even said that the earth actually rests on a gigantic double vajra i.e. in symbolic terms, this Reality underlies all of existence.

These two vajras, crossed, also represent the total integration of all the energies - psychological, emotional, physical, etc. - that would be experienced by an Enlightened being. We often talk about people being quite "together"; in other words, reasonably integrated: they are reliable, kind, know themselves pretty well, don't do strange and unpredictable things or fly off the handle etc. You could say the double vajra symbolises what it would be like to be a cosmically, unimaginably "together" person! Completely unencumbered by self-doubt, confusion or subconscious tendencies, you would be able to achieve virtually anything. And this is what Amoghasiddhi's name means: unobstructed success.

The Buddha taught that ALL unenlightened people were mad, in the sense that we don't see life as it really is, as I've already described. As a child and adult, I have experienced a lot of mental illness and confusion in people close to me and found this very disturbing; it affected my confidence and sometimes I didn't know which way was up. But sometimes in my mind's eye, in meditation, I have seen Amoghasiddhi's double vajra glowing, almost flaming, in the darkness; a symbol of total sanity, clarity and hope, inspiring me to continue fearlessly, have faith in myself and trust my judgement; and reminding me that total sanity does exist and it may take me a long time, but I am on the way to it."

Seminar topic

What does Catherine mean when she points out that it is said that the earth rests on a double-vajra?

For reflection

Could you describe you, or any of your friends, as 'together'? If so why? If not what qualities would you/they need to develop?

Catherine has chosen to think of Amoghasiddhi's qualities, to help her to try to develop those same qualities within herself. This is a typical Buddhist practice. If you wanted to change and develop, whose qualities might you contemplate? Why?

How are these beings understood?

Some Mahayana Buddhists think of these beings as really existing in a time and space separated from our own, yet available to us in the here and now. As bodhisattvas, they have, out of compassion, postponed their final entry into nirvana in order to help all suffering beings to attain enlightenment. As such, Buddhists may ask them for assistance on the path. For example, those who follow the tradition of devotion to Amida say that they need only call on him when they despair of ever reaching enlightenment by their own efforts, and he will ensure their birth in the Pure Land.

For other Mahayanists, these figures represent aspects of enlightenment to which they aspire. For example, a Buddhist who wishes to develop compassion may contemplate the figure of Avalokitesvara, with his many heads and many arms. The heads show his superhuman awareness of the sufferings of all beings, and his many arms show his great capacity for compassionate acts. Buddhists believe that by contemplating, or thinking about, compassion in this way, it is possible to develop it in oneself.

And the historical Buddha?

The historical Buddha (usually referred to as Shakyamuni in Mahayana Buddhism) is seen as no more and no less important than other enlightened beings. Like a Bodhisattva he did not remain in the bliss of nirvana under the bodhi-tree but, out of compassion, he re-engaged with the world to teach people the way out of suffering.

In a form of Japanese Buddhism called Nichiren Buddhism, which uses the Lotus Sutra as its scripture, the Buddha is seen not as a historical person. He is rather seen as representing the principle of Buddhahood, or of ultimate reality. Buddhism always links the Buddha with his teachings, the Dharma. In the Lotus Sutra they are seen as the same thing. To put it another way, the Buddha is the same thing as the Truth, or the way things really are. The Buddha is not so much a person, as the force of truth, which is always there.

Another form of Buddhism, called Zen, sees concepts and ideas like those found in the scriptures, as potential distractions from the path of enlightenment. The Ninth Century Chinese Zen master Lin chi famously said that 'If you come across the Buddha in your path, kill him.' This kind of talk is designed to shock people into realising that they might be developing attachments to teachers, or to ideas that, though religious, are actually preventing them from experiencing the truth.

A summary of the different ways the Buddha is perceived

Theravada	Mahayana
There is only one Buddha	There are many Buddhas
The Buddha is a human being	There are celestial Buddhas/ the Buddha represents ultimate reality
The Buddha is an example	As well as being examples, enlightened beings help others to attain enlightenment
Attaining Enlightenment is a rare thing	Everybody has the Buddha-nature, and Buddha-hood is a possibility

Chapter 4

This statue of the Buddha is at Amaravati Monastery in Hertfordshire. Is it surprising to see snow on a statue of the Buddha? Perhaps this is because we forget how far Buddhism has spread, and how diverse it has become.

Tasks

Research task	Using the internet and other sources, find information on the following enlightened beings, and make a presentation to the class explaining the symbolism in their iconography: **Aksobhya** **Amoghasiddhi** **Vairocana** **Ratnasambhava** **Amitabha** **Tara**
Writing tasks	Explore the connection between wisdom and compassion. Evaluate the view that Buddhists worship the Buddha. How might it help a Buddhist to 'visualise' an enlightened being. Was Lin chi's attitude to the Buddha disrespectful? Explain the different ways that the concept of 'Buddha' is understood within Buddhism. Evaluate the view that the Mahayana understanding of buddhahood is a corruption of proper Buddhism.

Glossary

Aksobhya	One of the five dhyani Buddhas. His name means 'imperturbable' and he is associated with the colour blue.
Amoghasiddhi	One of the five dhyani Buddhas. His name means 'unobstructed success' and he is associated with the colour green.
Avalokitsevara	The bodhisattva of compassion. His name means 'he who hears the cries of the world.'
Bodhisattva	Literally 'Enlightenment being'. In the Mahayana tradition, a being who has postponed entry into nirvana in order to assist others.
Buddhahood	A state that Mahayana Buddhists would say is available to everybody.
Buddha-nature	Mahayana Buddhism describes every being as having a latent Buddha-nature, that needs to be revealed.
Celestial Buddhas	Buddhas that occupy realms other than our human realm.
Compassion	One of the two principle characteristics of a Buddha or Bodhisattva, the other being Wisdom.
Manjusri	The bodhisattva of wisdom.
Nichiren Buddhism	A form of Japanese Buddhism that sees the Lotus Sutra as the most authoritative scripture.
Pratitya Samutpada / Paticca Samuppada	Often translated as 'Conditioned Co-production, 'Interdependent Origination'. A description of reality, denoting that all phenomena are causally linked.
Ratnasambhava	One of the five dhyani Buddhas. His name means 'jewel-born one' and he is associated with the colour yellow.
Samsara	The endless round of birth, death and rebirth and entrapment in dukkha.
Tara	A female enlightened being, venerated by Tibetan Buddhists.
Vairocana	One of the five dhyani buddhas. His name means 'the illuminator' and he is associated with the colour white.
Vishva-vajra	The double thunderbolt, representing the impact of enlightenment a thousand times over.
Wisdom	One of the two principle characteristics of a Buddha or Bodhisattva, the other being Compassion.
Zen	A form of Japanese Mahayana Buddhism that emphasises that nirvana is in the here and now.

Concepts and Practices

Aim of the Section

This section first focuses on key teachings attributed to the Buddha, and on the philosophical underpinnings of the religion as a whole. During the discussion of the key teachings it is important to consider how you might explore and illustrate them, and ways in which you can put them into your own words.

Second, it explores the ways in which Buddhists practise their beliefs. Here there will be focus on the importance of the Sangha, or community; on the noble eightfold path; and on two practices most associated with Buddhism - meditation and puja. It will be important for you to think about how these practices, and the life of the community, reflect Buddhist beliefs.

During your study of this section it is important to be aware that Buddhism is a diverse religion, containing numerous different beliefs and practices.

The Three Marks of Existence and the Four Noble Truths

Aim

In this chapter you will gain knowledge about the Buddhist description of the human condition, and understanding of its implications. You should be able to respond to the teachings of the three marks of existence and the four noble truths, and be able to show through use of examples and illustrations that you understand what is meant by them.

The Dharma

The teachings of Buddhism are known as the dhamma (P) dharma (Skt). This word means 'teachings' or 'truth'. The words of the Buddha are considered to be the dharma, but also any teaching that helps on the way to enlightenment is thought of as the dharma. Buddhists consider the dharma to be as important as the Buddha himself. As mentioned earlier, the Buddha is reported to have said 'He who sees the dharma sees me, he who sees me sees the dharma.' Along with 'Buddha' and 'Dharma', Buddhists consider the 'Sangha' as the three important foundations of the religion.

The Three Marks of Existence: *The Lakshanas*

One of the first things the Buddha did after he had become enlightened, was to set out what he saw as the human condition. According to Buddhists there are only three things of which we can be completely sure. We cannot know whether the world was created by God, whether there is life after death or anything like that. All we can be sure about is that existence has these three qualities:

Dukkha (P) /duhkha (Skt)	suffering/unsatisfactoriness
Anicca (P) /anitya (Skt)	impermanence
Anatta (P) /anatman (Skt)	no permanent self

For reflection

Is there anything in life that you can be completely sure of?

Dukkha

Dukkha is an extremely difficult word to translate. Most often, it is translated as suffering, but a number of scholars of Buddhism warn us that this is not its only meaning. Walpola Rahula describes this translation as 'highly unsatisfactory and misleading. It is because', he says, 'of this limited, free and easy translation, and its superficial interpretation, that many people have been misled into regarding Buddhism as pessimistic.'[3] John Snelling in his Buddhist handbook alerts us to the fact that the term has 'a wide spectrum' of meanings:

'At one extreme,' he says, 'it takes in the most dire forms of mental and physical pain: the agonies of cancer, for instance, and the anguish of someone who falls prey to total despair. It covers our everyday aches and pains, our petty dislikes and frustrations too; and it extend to very subtle feelings of malaise; that life is never quite right.'[4]

Dukkha is in fact a description of the human condition. It touches everything, even happiness. The Buddha never denied that it was possible to be happy in life (in fact, he himself had been very happy whilst in his father's palace), he just denied that this happiness was eternal. Because no happiness is ever permanent, all happiness is 'tainted.'

The best way to try to understand this is to think of examples from your own life. When were you at your most happy? Was it during a perfect holiday, or at a pop concert, or on a walk in the countryside? A time spent with family, friends, a special person? Think about this time. No doubt about it, you were extremely happy! But the question the Buddha would ask is, were you perfectly happy?

As you try to remember the feelings of happiness at that time, are there any other feelings that creep in? Even the best times come to an end. A wonderful holiday can be a bitter-sweet experience. Even if you are in the place of your dreams, doing the things you love to do, with the people you love to be with (which is a tall order in itself!) with everyday that passes, the holiday becomes shorter, and you are one day nearer returning to the drudgery of ordinary life and that familiar Monday morning feeling. In fact the dread of Monday morning can be even worse when you are having a wonderful time than it is under normal circumstances! That feeling of dread can just take the edge off your enjoyment. It taints it. This is not to say you don't enjoy the holiday, it may be the best time you ever had in your whole life, but it doesn't give you perfect, or what John Snelling calls 'unalloyed' happiness.

For reflection

What is happiness?

This 'taint' is dukkha. It does not mean suffering, it just means the absence of total, perfect, unalloyed happiness. Dukkha is not only about good things coming to an end. It is about everything being fundamentally imperfect, even if only slightly. A more helpful translation may be the coinage 'unsatisfactoriness', but it is always important to 'unpack' the meaning of this. After all, the Buddha said that dukkha touches everything that exists – it is a 'mark', or 'quality' or 'characteristic' of existence. This means it is a fundamental philosophical concept requiring a great deal of explanation.

For reflection

Can you think of any times in your own life in which you have been aware of dukkha? In what ways are you experiencing dukkha now?

Seminar topic

What examples would you use to explain the concept of dukkha to someone who had never heard of it before?

Most religions say that although things in creation are not permanent, some things are eternal, like the soul, or god, or 'eternal life'. How do you think a Buddhist would respond to such ideas?

Anicca/ Anitya – Impermanence

This is the second of the three things that, according to Buddhists, we can be sure is true. Buddhists see all things (people, objects, states of mind, relationships, qualities, everything!) as being dependent on causes and conditions, and are therefore constantly changing. Nothing remains forever.

A good example of this is the flowers often placed by Buddhists on their shrines. Real flowers don't exist forever. They are obviously dependent on water for their existence, and if this dries up (which it does, as water evaporates – it is not stable, it is constantly changing) then the conditions for the flower's existence change and it decays. A flower is a good example of the transience of all things, because a flower perceptibly changes and decays. Buddhism says that this transience is a feature of all things. A plastic flower might seem to have the ability to last forever, but actually it is decaying too, just much more slowly than the real flower. Even the things that seem most solid, like land or mountains, are in fact in flux (or constant change).

Anatta/Anatman – no permanent self

When the Buddha said that everything is impermanent, he meant everything, including the self. Most religions argue that the soul, or the inner spark or essence of the person, is eternal. The religion in which the Buddha was brought up talked about the atman, or eternal and unchanging 'self'. However, the Buddha argued that it was a mistake to think in this way. The self, he argued, was dependent on the coming together of five 'skandhas' or bundles, all of which are changing. These skandhas are Form (the body), Sensations, Perceptions, Mental formations (impulses and habits) and Consciousness. None of these could be described as the soul or the essence of the person, not even consciousness, because there is no consciousness unless it is consciousness of something (i.e. consciousness is by no means permanent or unchanging, so therefore could not be considered to be the soul). Because the self is dependent on these five changing skandhas, it is itself in flux, dependent and impermanent.

> **Seminar topic**
>
> *Do you think that the combination of skandhas is the best description of 'the self'?*

As well as denying eternalism (the idea that anything, such as the soul, goes on for ever), the Buddha also denied nihilism (the idea everything finishes at death). The Buddha said that the person was something more than the body (i.e. he wasn't a materialist) or to put it another way, the skandha 'Form' is not the essential person. Therefore the person's life is not 'over' at the point of the death of their body. The body is just one skandha – all in are in flux, but the end of one does not mean the end of them all.

What about rebirth?

A metaphor often used to explain the relationship between one life and the next is the metaphor of the flame of a candle lighting the flame of another candle. Are the two flames the same flame? No, not exactly. But the first one is one of the causes of the second. Another metaphor is the relationship between milk and yoghurt. Are they the same thing? No, not exactly, but the milk is one of the causes of the yoghurt.
So the Buddhist idea of rebirth is that a life lived will provide the causes of another life (or of nirvana). The link is a causal one, rather than a substantial one (such as in the case of eternal atman occupying body after body).

Chapter 5

Buddhists are often asked the question, 'If there is no-self, who is it that achieves enlightenment?'

Sometimes this question comes from a misunderstanding that Buddhists say there is no-self whatsoever. They don't say that. They say that there is no fixed or permanent self. There is a person there, but that person is in flux – always changing.

What features of this person changed? Have any remained the same? Will they remain the same forever?

Lots of examples are given to explain this, such as the statement 'you can never step in the same river twice' made by the Greek philosopher Heraclitus, whose ideas were very similar to those of the Buddha. If you think about it, it is true, even though it doesn't seem to be so at first. Similarly, a person at one point in their life, is not exactly the same as they are a year later. Buddhists would point out that of course there might be some continuity between the person last year and the person this year, but you could not say it was exactly the same person. In fact, a person's life is like a piece of rope. The threads that make it up may be of different lengths, some very short indeed, but when it is woven together it appears to be a single, continuous strand. If you analysed the rope you would see it was made of short threads, just as if you analysed the self you would see it was made by ever-changing skandhas. Analysing the self is something Buddhists do when they meditate.

For reflection

Consider one of your childhood memories. Does it feel as if it happened to you, or to someone else? How would your feelings about that memory help to illustrate anatta?

Another example used to help explain the notion of anatta is the film strip:

If you watched this film, you would see what appeared to be continuous action. However, if you analysed it you would discover that this was an illusion created by still pictures. You see one picture, and then it's gone, then you see another, then it's gone. The self is like this. It appears to be continuous, but that appearance of continuity is dependent on things that are continually passing out of existence.

Reading Nagasena and the Chariot

The following is a passage from the Questions of King Menander (Milinda) (The Milindapanha), which is an account in Pali of a discussion of a Greek King (the Greeks ruled part of India from the third century BCE onwards. King Menander lived in the second century BCE).

King Menander greeted the Venerable Nagasena, and the King asked him, 'How are you known, what is your name?'

'I'm known as Nagasena, your Majesty, that is what my fellow monks call me. But though my parents may have given me such a name…it's only a generally understood term, a practical designation. There is no question of a permanent individual implied in the use of the word.'

The King replied, 'If that is the case, and there is no permanent individuality, who gives you monks your robes and food, lodging and medicines? And who makes use of them? Who lives a life of righteousness, meditates and reaches nirvana? If someone were to kill you there would be no question of murder'.

'If your fellow monks call you Nagasena, what then is Nagasena? Would you say that your hair is Nagasena?' said the King.

'No your majesty,' replied Nagasena.

'Or your nails, teeth, skin, or other parts of your body, or the outward form or sensation, or perception, or the psychic constructions or consciousness? Are any of these Nagasena?'

'No your majesty' . . .

'Then for all my asking, I find no Nagasena. Nagasena is a mere sound. Surely what your reverence has said is false!'

Then the venerable Nagasena addressed the King.

'Your Majesty, how did you come here – on foot or in a vehicle?

'In a chariot'.

'Then tell me what is the chariot? Is the pole the chariot?'

'No your reverence, ' said the King.

'Or the axle, wheels, frame, reins, yoke spokes or goad?'

'None of these things is the chariot.'

'Then is the chariot something other than the separate parts?'

'No your reverence.'

'Then for all my asking, your Majesty, I can find no chariot. The chariot is a mere sound. What then is the chariot? Surely what your Majesty has said is false! There is no chariot!, . . .

'What I said was not false,' replied the King. 'It is on account of all these various components, the pole, axle, wheels and so on, that the vehicle is called a chariot. It's just a practically understood term, a practical designation.'

'Well said, your Majesty! You know what the word chariot means! And it is just the same with me. It is on account of the various components of my being that I am known by the generally understood term, the practical designation, Nagasena.'

Adapted from the translation by Merv Fowler [5]

Seminar topics

Explain what Nagasena was trying to communicate to the King.

What do Buddhists mean when they say that the self is dependent on causes and conditions?

Explain why Buddhism is neither eternalistic nor nihilistic.

The Four Noble Truths

The Buddha taught the Four Noble Truths in his first sermon at the Deer Park, Isipatana.

They are

> **1) Dukkha**
>
> **2) Samudaya (the arising of dukkha)**
>
> **3) Nirodha (the cessation of dukkha)**
>
> **4) Magga (the way)**

These truths are usually explained as follows:

All life is dukkha.

Dukkha is caused by tanha ('thirst', desire, attachment, craving).

Tanha can be overcome, therefore dukkha can be overcome.

Tanha can be overcome by following the path.

Another traditional way in which they are expressed is: 'The Disease, the Cause, the Cure, the Medicine'.[6]

Man Yao is a Taiwanese Ch'an (Zen) nun. She became a nun in 1986 when she was 24, and was given her dharma name, Man Yao, which means 'fully shining'. Before becoming a nun she had been a successful businesswoman, involved in the import-export industry. Her decision to become a nun was based on her realisation that 'money does not perfect your mind.'

The first truth is also the first lakshana, or mark of existence (see page 27). It is the Buddhist description of the human condition, or to put it another way, it is the diagnosis of the 'illness' from which we all suffer. It is what is wrong. Buddhists see this analysis as neither pessimistic nor optimistic. It is simply realistic. The recognition that all life is dukkha, is the first step in the way to overcoming it.

The positive thrust of Buddhism comes from the subsequent three truths. Not only is the problem diagnosed, but a cause is identified, and a cure is at hand. All conditioned things have a cause, and dukkha is caused by tanha, which literally translates as thirst, though it is more usually explained with terms such as 'attachment' or 'craving'. It is easy to acquire a superficial understanding of the relationship between tanha and dukkha, but according to Buddhists, it is the work of possibly many lifetimes to understand it fully. An easy example is that of greed for what money can buy.

It is a cliché that money cannot buy happiness, and rich people (especially if they are greedy) can be amongst the most miserable. Buddhists would say it is our greed that creates our dissatisfaction. We want ever more, bigger and better, and suffer because of our lack. We are never satisfied with what we have and constantly crave for more. This state is superbly depicted by the example of the hungry ghost (preta), in the diagram of the Wheel of Life (see page 42). The large belly indicates their overwhelming appetites, their small mouths and necks, their inability to ever satisfy themselves. They are plagued by raging thirst, but can drink only from flaming and infested waters.

Seminar topic

The realm of the hungry ghosts is sometimes thought of as another dimension of existence, and it is sometimes thought of as a metaphor for states into which humans can fall for a period of time. How effective is it as a metaphor?

However, material desire is only one of the many forms of tanha, and is perhaps one of the most easy to deal with. Other forms of attachment include attachment to people, or to particular beliefs. On the surface it may seem a good thing to be attached to people, but Buddhism says these attachments are unhelpful if they are defined by what you can get out of them. If they are 'giving' relationships, then they are positive. If they are 'taking' relationships, then they are negative and feed dukkha.

Seminar topic

Can a Buddhist ever justify being in love?

Attachment to particular beliefs is also a dukkha-causing form of tanha. The Buddhist understanding of the Middle Way is not only about avoiding extremes of luxury and asceticism; it is also about avoiding extreme views about the nature of existence, such as nihilism or eternalism, or whether there is a creator, or whether there is life after death. It seems that the Buddha classed these views as metaphysical speculation.

They are speculation because we cannot prove them one way or the other, and even if we could, it would not help in the struggle to overcome dukkha . This idea is illustrated by the parable of the poisoned arrow.

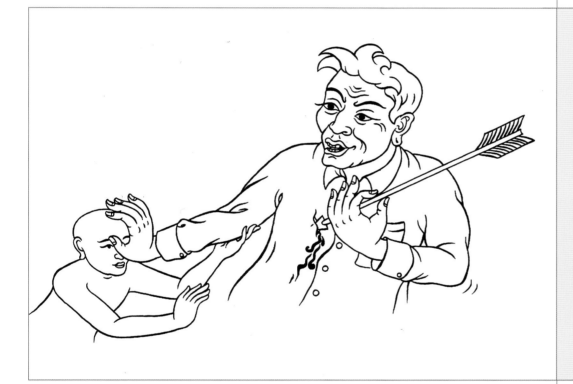

The Human Condition: Our suffering needs an urgent cure, but instead of accepting help we indulge in speculation, which only serves to increase our distress.

The Parable of the Poisoned Arrow

It is as if there was a man struck by an arrow that was smeared thickly with poison; his friends and relatives would summon a doctor. And the man might say, 'I will not draw out this arrow as long as I do not know whether the man by whom I was struck was a Brahmin, a Kshatriya, a Vaishya or a Shudra....as long as I don't know his name and his family .... whether he was tall, short or of medium height...' That man would not discover these things, but that man would die.

Majjhima Nikaya i. 429 Adapted from translation in Gethin, Rupert, The Foundations of Buddhism, Oxford, OPUS, 1998

As well as these attachments, there is also the attachment to one's idea of oneself. This attachment takes many forms. It can involve attachment to the body, or to ideas about one's own prosperity or success. The following passage from the Sutta Nipata, explains graphically why vanity about one's physical appearance is irrational, and makes the problem of attachment worse.

Some Buddhists consider it helpful to meditate on the transient and unpleasant nature of the body, and many Buddhist temples own skeletons so that people can sit and contemplate them. Buddhists also warn that this type of practice can be unhelpful and even dangerous for someone who is depressed or has an overly negative view of the body anyway. As always in Buddhism, a teaching is only worthwhile if it actually helps to eliminate craving.

Reading On the Body

For as the body when dead is repulsive, so it is also when it is alive; but on account of the concealment afforded by adornment, its repulsiveness escapes notice. The body is in reality a collection of over three hundred bones, and is framed into a whole by means of one hundred and eighty joints. It is held together by nine hundred tendons, and overlaid by nine-hundred muscles, and has an outside envelope of moist cuticle covered by an epidermis full of pores, through which there is an incessant oozing and trickling, as if from a kettle of fat. It is prey to vermin, the seat of disease, and subject to all manner of miseries. Through its nine orifices it is always discharging matter, like a ripe boil. Matter is secreted from the two eyes, wax from the ears, snot from the nostrils, and from the mouth issue food, bile, phlegm and blood, and from the two lower orifices of the body faeces and urine, while from the ninety-nine thousand pores of the skin an unclean sweat exudes, attracting black flies and other insects ... However, when, with the help of tooth-sticks, mouth-rinses, and various ablutions, men have cleansed their teeth, the rest of their persons, and with manifold garments have covered their nakedness, and have anointed themselves with many-coloured and fragrant unguents, and adorned themselves with flowers and ornaments, they find themselves able to believe in 'I' and a 'mine'. Accordingly it is on account of the concealment afforded by this adornment that people fail to recognize the essential repulsiveness of their bodies, and that men find pleasure in women and women in men. In reality, however, there is not the smallest just reason for being pleased.

A proof of this is the fact that when any part of the body becomes detached, as, for instance, the hair of the head, hair of the body, nails, teeth, phlegm, snot, faeces or urine, people are unwilling so much as to touch it, and are distressed at, ashamed of, and loathe it. But in respect of what remains, though that is likewise repulsive, yet men are so wrapped in blindness, and infatuated by a passionate fondness for their own selves that they believe it to be something desirable, lovely, lasting, pleasant and an Ego.

Suttanipata I;11, v1-14, from Whitfield Foy's, Man's Religious Quest, London, The Open University Press, 1978 pp210-211

Seminar topic

Do you think that the Buddha's teaching on this matter is too extreme? Do you think it might be helpful for some people? How would thinking in this way about the body help to develop detachment?

The third noble truth, known as 'nirodha' or cessation, is that tanha can be overcome, and therefore dukkha can be overcome. This is sometimes described as 'the good news' of Buddhism, and is a truth that derives from the Buddhist view of connectedness, sometimes stated in the formula 'When this arises, that arises. When this ceases, that ceases.' Release from dukkha does not mean that physical pain no longer occurs. It means that the psychological suffering that often comes along with physical pain does not arise (i.e. that it does not lead to further craving). Someone who has perfected non-attachment lives just like anyone else, except that they no longer experience the dukkha associated with craving and ignorance.

The fourth truth, known as 'magga' or 'way', contains the teachings designed to root out craving, ignorance, greed and hatred, and so providing the conditions for enlightenment. Sometimes the teachings are formularised into the Noble Eightfold Path, a discussion of which begins on page 45, but it is important to remember that Buddhism takes many forms, and 'the way' is described differently by Buddhists of different traditions.

a discussion of which begins on page 45

Tasks

Writing tasks	Explain why 'suffering' is an unsatisfactory translation of the term dukkha.
	Explain how the parable of the poisoned arrow illustrates possible distractions from the quest for enlightenment.
	'Buddhists are wrong when they say that questions about creation and life after death are merely speculation.' Assess the validity of this view.
Play	Write and perform a play that illustrates the Four Noble Truths.
Survey	Design a multiple choice questionnaire, to be answered anonymously by your classmates, that ascertains their views about the relevance of the four noble truths today..
	Present your findings in a pie-chart or bar-chart format.

For reflection

What would you find easier: giving up your material possessions (all of them, bar the shirt on your back and a begging bowl), or giving up a world-view, or cherished beliefs, or fanaticism about a pop group or rugby/football team, or an attachment to a particular person?

Chapter 5

Glossary

anatta/anatman	No-self', the view that there is nothing about the person that persists eternally, without change. One of the three lakshanas.
anicca/anitya	'Impermanence.' One of the three lakshanas.
dukkha	The human condition. There is no satisfactory equivalent in English or Welsh, and it is often translated as 'unsatisfactoriness', 'suffering', 'frustration'. It is the first of the Four Noble Truths and one of the three lakshanas.
eternalism	The belief that the soul will persist forever. (Buddhists are not eternalists).
lakshanas	The three marks of existence: anatta, anicca, and dukkha.
magga	'The way' – the Noble Eightfold Path.
materialism	The belief that the person is made only of the body. (Buddhists are not materialists).
Milindapanha	An important Pali text, known in English as the 'Questions of King Milinda.'
Nagasena	The Buddhist monk who engages in dialogue with King Milinda in the Milindapanha.
nihilism	The belief that when the body dies, the person dies.
nirodha	'Cessation' – the third of the Four Noble Truths, that craving and therefore dukkha can be overcome.
preta	Hungry ghosts. One of the realms depicted on the bhavacakra.
samudaya	'Origin' – the second of the Four Noble Truths, that craving is the origin of dukkha.
skandhas	The five 'aggregates' that make up the human being.
tanha	Craving, thirst, attachment.

Rebirth and Interconnectedness

Aim

After studying this chapter you should be able to demonstrate your understanding of the Buddhist teachings of karma and rebirth, and of the way in which the bhavachakra (Wheel of Life) illustrates the teaching of Pratitya Samutpada (interdependent origination, or interconnectedness.) You should also be able to critically evaluate the validity of these teachings.

Indian thought at the time of the Buddha saw the soul or self (atman) as being trapped in samsara, the cycle of birth, death and rebirth, driven on by the power of karma to experience reincarnation after reincarnation. The nature of each reincarnation, and the experiences of each lifetime, were as much the result of behaviour in previous lives, as in the current lifespan.

The opening two verses of the famous Buddhist scripture, the Dhammapada, seem to imply the same sort of belief. They speak of a causal (karmic) link between pure and impure intentions and the experience of joy or suffering as the inevitable effect.

The Dhammapada

1   What we are today comes from our thoughts of yesterday, and our present thoughts build our life of tomorrow: our life is the creation of our mind.
If a man speaks or acts with an impure mind, suffering follows him as the wheel of the cart follows the beast that draws the cart.

2   What we are today comes from our thoughts of yesterday, and our present thoughts build our life of tomorrow: our life is the creation of our mind.
If a man speaks or acts with a pure mind, joy follows him as his own shadow.

Trans Juan Mascaro, The Dhammapada Harmondsworth, Penguin, 1973, p35

Seminar topic

What does this passage from the Dhammapada say about the importance of people's intentions?

However, key to the Buddhist understanding of reality is the belief that there is no permanent or fixed self (anatta/anatman) (see page 29). So, although Buddhists believe in a connection between cause and effect (karma), as is clearly demonstrated in the Dhammapada, they do not believe that there is total continuity between one life and the next. This is why Buddhists tend not to use the term reincarnation. Literally, reincarnation means 'becoming flesh again,' and implies the entry of a soul into a sequence of bodily existences. To put it another way, the same individual is born, lives, dies, and is born again into another body.

Broadly speaking, reincarnation is a Hindu belief. Buddhists, on the other hand, would use the term rebirth. Buddhist are not eternalists (unlike Hindus), but nor are they nihilists (unlike secular humanists). They do not believe a permanent soul exists forever (since all the skandhas are in flux), but neither do they believe that physical death is the end. After

The two flames are not the same, but the first provided the cause for the second

Seminar topic

In what ways are you the same person now as you were when you were three years old? Apart from being older, how are you different now? To what extent will you be the same person as you are now when you are twenty-five, and when you are sixty?

How do Buddhists explain the relationship between one life and the next?

Why are some people afraid of growing old? How will you cope with old age? Why do Buddhists try not to worry about old age?

all, 'form' or the physical body is only one of the skandhas. Buddhists believe that one life is caused by the next in the same way that a flame from a candle causes a second flame, or in the same way that the momentum of one snooker ball is the cause of the movement of the next.

The two flames are not the same, but the first provided the cause for the second. So the person in one life is both continuous with, yet different from, the person in the next life. This continuity and difference is also a feature within one life-span (remember the image of the film strip?). It could be said that we die to the last moment, and are reborn into this moment. In other words, I am not 'the same' person as I was a moment ago. Rebirth is an ongoing process that characterises all life. The death of the physical body marks just one change amongst many that have occurred, moment to moment, across lifetimes. Rebirth with a new physical body is no more or less significant than rebirth into the next moment.

The notion of rebirth contains within it both the idea of constant change and the idea of connectedness through causation. Whilst I may not be the same person I was a moment ago, the person I am now was 'caused' by the person I was a moment ago. This causation is known in Buddhism as karma.

The idea that one thing causes another is fundamental to Buddhism, and is often expressed as the teaching of pratitya samutpada (P. paticca samuppada). This term is translated in a variety of different ways, such as 'interdependent origination', 'conditioned co-production', or 'dependent arising'. Pratitya samutpada is just the way things are, i.e. related or connected to each other. Again the formula 'when this arises that arises, when this ceases that ceases' is used to describe this.

Another way in which this teaching is expressed is in the Tibetan 'Wheel of Life' or 'Bhavacakra'. This is also sometimes called the 'Wheel of Becoming', or the 'Wheel of Samsara'

The Wheel is held by Yama, the god of death. In fact he is sometimes described as either eating or spewing the wheel, showing that everything is subject, ultimately, to death. In Japanese tradition, the god of death holds up a mirror to those who arrive in his realm, in which they see not only their lives replayed, but also the ways in which their deeds had consequences for others. For some, this could be described as hell itself.

Task

Writing task	Write a short story or film script about the effects of someone's life being shown to them by Yama.

In this classic piece of iconography, the mirror is held up to all existence.

The Twelve Links

The outer circle shows the twelve links. These are a way of expressing the truth that ignorance about the consequences of things leads inevitably to suffering. The symbolism of the twelve links is ancient and difficult to understand, and it is important not to take the pictures literally. For example, the pictures of the pregnant woman and the woman giving birth have little to do with the actual birth of children. They are symbols for 'becoming' or 'arising' – the idea that one thing leads to another, so grasping leads to becoming, which results in the fruition of karma, and therefore inevitably to suffering and decay.

The pictures are:

1. *a blind man* (ignorance), 2. *a potter making a pot* (formations), 3. *a monkey picking fruit* (consciousness), 4. *a boat on a journey* (mind and body), 5. *a house with six windows* (the six senses – Buddhists include the mind as a sense), 6. *a couple embracing* (sense contact), 7. *a man with an arrow in his eye* (feeling), 8. *a man drinking* (thirst), 9. *a man picking fruit* (grasping), 10. *a pregnant woman* (becoming), 11. *a woman in labour* (rebirth, i.e. the fruition of karma), 12. *a man carrying a corpse to a cremation ground* (old age and death).

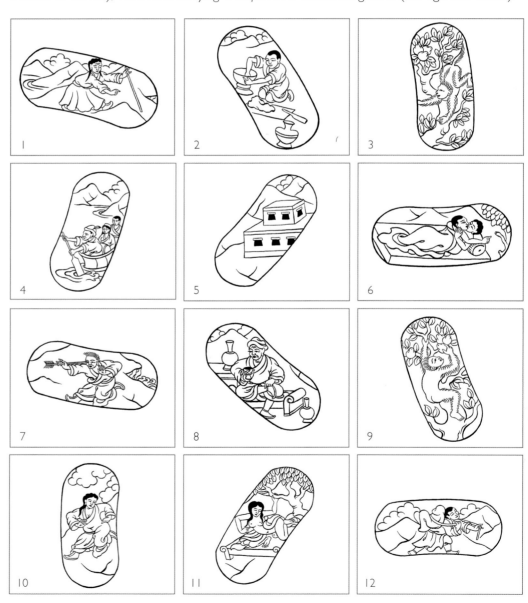

The Six Realms

The next circle in shows six realms of rebirth. They are (at the top) the realm of the gods, and then (moving clockwise) the realm of the jealous gods, the realm of animals, the realm of the hells, the realm of the hungry ghosts and finally the human realm. Buddhists believe that our human realm is not the only realm or dimension, and that the universe contains within it many other modes of existence. For example the Buddha encounters numerous beings from the realm of the gods during his teaching career. Gods are not seen as perfect beings in Buddhism. They too are subject to dukkha, just much less so than humans. In fact, birth as a human is preferable to birth as a god because in the human existence enough suffering is experienced to spur us on in the quest for enlightenment.

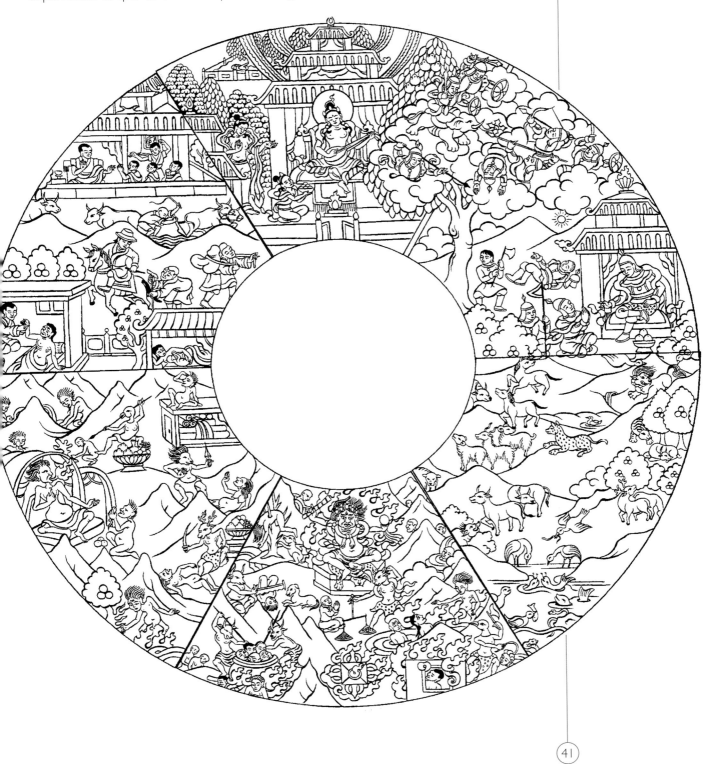

Chapter 6

The realms are sometimes seen as physically different existences into which rebirth of the physical body might occur. At the same time they are also seen as states of being or states of mind into which it is possible to be reborn (i.e. within the same life span). For example, the Buddha's life prior to his renunciation could be described as life in the realm of the gods. He lived a life in which he did not experience or perceive decay and suffering. Buddhists might say that our comfortable lives in the west are very much like the lives of the gods. After all we are, for the most part, successful at turning our faces away from the sufferings of most of the world in order to pursue our own happiness, and do quite well at avoiding the realities of sickness, old age and death. Alternatively they might say that the realms reflect our own lives. For example, at our happiest moments we might be said to be in the realm of the gods; or when we are driven only by instinct we could be said to be in the realm of the animals; or when we are in torment and fear we could be said to be in the hell realm.

Seminar topic

Consider evidence for the argument that our society tends not to face up to the realities of sickness, old age and death.

Seminar topic

Do you think some people deserve to remain in the realm of hells forever? Why/why not?

None of the realms are seen as permanent. No-one, for instance, is damned to hell eternally, nor is the realm of the gods a permanent abode (such as it would be in some other religions). The only permanent state in Buddhism is nirvana. Everything else is subject to change (anicca/anitya).

For reflection

Think of the six realms as six states of mind. Which ones are you in most of the time?

The realm of the hungry ghosts is a particularly unpleasant place. The picture shows creatures with large stomachs, but with thin necks and tiny mouths. This is clearly to indicate the idea of massive but insatiable appetites! The idea of 'appetite' is very close to the Buddhist idea of tanha or craving, and the notion of being perpetually in a state of terrible craving sums up what, at times, it feels like to be a human being. In some Buddhists countries the hungry ghosts are thought of as tormented spirits, and food is put out for them as a gesture of kindness.

Moving inwards again on the Wheel, we see beings rising on the left and falling on the right. This is a pictorial representation of karma, the idea that good actions inevitably result in good effects, and bad actions inevitably result in bad effects.

The Three Fires

At the axle of the hub of the wheel there are three animals. The cockerel symbolises greed, the snake, hatred, and the pig, ignorance. These three aspects of life are sometimes called the three fires or the three poisons, and they are what keeps the wheel of samsara turning. They drive us on to experience more and more dukkha. Greed and hatred are two sides of the same coin – 'I want' and 'I don't want'. Therefore they are both forms of grasping and craving. (Craving to get away from, or to get out of something, is just as much craving as desiring to have something else). Ignorance (Skt. avidya) is not knowing that greed and hatred lead to dukkha. To put it another way, it is ignorance of pratitya samutpada - the truth that all things in samsara are the result of a cause, and that all things are linked or connected.

Tasks

Writing task	Explain the Buddhist understanding of the six realms of rebirth.
	Assess the view that Buddhist believe in life after death.
Research task	Collect evidence from newspapers and the internet that demonstrates that the three fires are the cause of suffering. You will need to write a short commentary on each item to explain the link. Consider ways in which you could present your findings (in a scrap book – as a wall display?) Did you find any examples of suffering that are not caused by greed, hatred and ignorance? How might Buddhists explain this?

Glossary

avidya	Ignorance or delusion.
Bhavacakra	The Wheel of Life.
Dhammapada	A popular portion of the Pali Canon.
nirvana	'Blowing out', the goal and highest attainment for Buddhists. This term is often defined negatively to avoid the problem of attempting to define something that cannot be defined. It is often described as the cessation or 'blowing out' of greed, hatred, ignorance, attachment and egoism. It is sometimes seen as the opposite of samsara and dukkha. It is often spoken of as synonymous with enlightenment. Different traditions of Buddhism define it in different ways.
three fires / poisons	Greed, hatred and ignorance – the three qualities that keep the unenlightened locked in the endless round of samsara.

Eightfold Path

The Buddhist life is governed by a set of ethical and practical principles, known as the Noble Eightfold Path.

The eightfold path is in fact the fourth of the four noble truths – 'magga' (the way). It sets out the aspects of life to which the Buddhist must attend in order to make progress, and to attain the 'Middle Way'. Each feature is worked on simultaneously. The eight aspects are not to be seen as eight steps. In fact, visualising the path as an eight-spoked wheel is much more helpful. Each spoke is necessary for the stability and integrity of the wheel.

Most books lay out the aspects of the path as 'right' this, or 'right' that. This is not to suggest that there is a right and wrong way of doing things, rather it is to suggest that each aspect can be better cultivated. Buddhists stress that the path is not to be seen as a set of commandments. The Buddha constantly told his followers that he was not issuing commandments, but showing them a way out of suffering, which they could take up if they found it useful, and discard if they did not.

The path's aspects can be grouped into three sections:

WISDOM (panna)	MORALITY (sila)	MEDITATION (samadhi)
Right understanding	Right speech	Right effort
Right thought	Right action	Right mindfulness
	Right livelihood	Right concentration

Right Understanding

This means understanding the Buddhist doctrines of impermanence and no-self. Obviously this is a task that might take lifetimes to perfect. Understanding the truth about the way things really are is different from our ordinary 'understanding'.

Right Thought

In Buddhism, not only actions but also thinking has karmic results. If, in our minds, we are hating or desiring, that will inevitably affect our actions in a negative way. If we purify our minds of hatred and desire, then no negative actions or suffering can follow.

Right Speech

If our minds are pure our speech will also be pure. Buddhists try to be very aware of the consequences of things that they say. Because everything is connected, and all actions have consequences, a careless word could cause damage, to others or to oneself. Buddhists try not to gossip, or to lie, or to be argumentative, or to indulge in the sort of speech that is really designed to inflate the self and put others down. Speech has always been considered very important in Buddhism – the Buddha spoke his teachings, sometimes known as Buddhavacanca (the words of the Buddha) and the teachings were preserved through recitation. Buddhists try to speak the dharma whenever it is appropriate.

Right Action

This involves taking the precepts (see page 51) and attempting to live by them. Right action is closely linked to right thought. An action can only be right if it is intended to be right. The intention is more important than the action itself. For example, giving food or gifts to a monastery would be considered right action. However, if someone gives a large amount, and someone else gives a small amount, there is no difference between the two gifts as the intention was the same.

Right Livelihood

There should be no occupation that brings harm to others. As well as avoiding certain kinds of work (e.g. the manufacture of arms or tobacco), Buddhists also try to set up businesses that work on ethical principals. The Friends of the Western Buddhist Order, for example run many such businesses, like craft shops that do not exploit workers in the developing world; cafés that sell only organically produced vegan food; ethical investment and legal advice, etc.

Seminar topic

Imagine you are setting up your own 'right livelihood' advertising company. What issues would you need to consider? (Do not think only of right livelihood, but other aspects of the eightfold path and of the precepts as well.)

Right Effort

Great commitment and effort is required on the quest for enlightenment. Greed, hatred and ignorance are very difficult indeed to overcome. Buddhists are often asked by critics of the religion whether they are 'attached' to the goal of nirvana, considering that all their efforts are directed towards attaining it.

They answer that desire is only bad if it is desire for oneself. The enlightened know that self is an illusion, and that only the enlightened can teach others the way out of suffering. So the desire for enlightenment is good, because it will benefit others. It is not wrong in Buddhism to have commitments or goals that are beneficial. The compassionate desire for world peace, for instance, would not be seen as a negative desire, and many Buddhists work hard to that end. However if the intention of such work is to seem good in the eyes of others, working for world peace would be seen as a negative attachment.

Right Mindfulness

Buddhists try to live in a state of mindfulness at all times. This means having an awareness of the consequences of thoughts, speech and actions, and to think, act and speak skilfully. It means being aware of one's inner motivations and intentions and trying to rid them of greed hatred and ignorance.

Right Concentration

This refers to the proper use of meditation to gain insight into the true nature of things, such as the self as a collection of the skandhas constantly in flux; the arising and ceasing of desires and delusion; and the connectedness of all beings and all aspects of the universe.

Tasks

Research task	Compare the Eightfold Path with rules from other religions. In what ways are they similar, and in what ways different?
Task	Choose one of the three aspects of the eightfold path and create a visual representation of it for use in contemplation. Use artwork, illustrations, photographs and computer generated representations.

In Theravada Buddhism, a great deal of attention is given to the eightfold path. In other forms of Buddhism, however, other teachings are used to assist the person in attaining enlightenment.

The Paramitas

Many Mahayana Buddhists try to keep the lay precepts (see page 51), but they also try to cultivate the six perfections or paramitas. These are positive qualities that will help the Buddhist on the path to enlightenment. They are Giving (dana), Morality (sila), Energy (virya), Patience (kshanti), Meditation (samadhi), Wisdom (prajna)

Seminar topic

Can you see any substantial differences between the paramitas and the eightfold path?

The Bodhisattva path

Mahayana Buddhists may also commit themselves to the Bodhisattva path, which is usually described as being in ten stages that are gone through over many lifetimes. The aim of the bodhisattva is to attain enlightenment for the sake of others. A vow to that effect is made at the beginning of the bodhisattva path. In this form of Buddhism it makes no sense to think of an individual attaining enlightenment by himself and for himself. In Mahayana Buddhism all beings are proceeding towards enlightenment, with the help of the bodhisattvas. This idea can be seen in the iconography of bodhisattvas.

Chapter 7

In this picture the Bodhisattva Amitabha looks over his shoulder in compassion for others struggling to attain release from suffering.

Task

Writing tasks	Explain the practical teachings of Buddhism designed to overcome craving and attachment. 'Living a religious life is much more to do with what you believe than following rules' Evaluate this view. Evaluate the view that the eightfold path provides a coherent ethical framework for life.
Research task	Discover Buddhist responses to controversial issues such as euthanasia, abortion, genetic engineering, vivisection for medical purposes, and war. How far are those responses informed by the precepts and the eightfold path?

Glossary

Buddhavacana	The words of the Buddha.
dana	Giving. One of the six paramitas.
Friends of the Western Buddhist Order	A movement founded in 1967 by an English Buddhist known as Sangharakshita.
kshanti	Patience. One of the six paramitas.
panna/prajna	Wisdom. One of the six paramitas.
paramitas	Positive qualities that the Mahayana Buddhist tries to develop.
samadhi	Meditation. One of the six paramitas.
sila	Morality. One of the six paramitas.
virya	Energy. One of the six paramitas.

The Sangha

Aim

After studying this chapter you should be able to demonstrate familiarity with the lifestyle of Sangha members, with the precepts, and with initiation practices. You should be able to describe the role of the Sangha within Buddhism, and to evaluate its importance. You should also understand the challenges of being a Sangha member in Wales.

The word Sangha has a strict meaning and a wider meaning. In its strict sense it refers to the order of Buddhist monks, but in its wide sense it refers to the whole community of practising Buddhists. The Sangha is one of the Three Jewels of Buddhism.

The Three Jewels

The Three Jewels (Skt, Triratna) are the three pillars of the Buddhist religion. They are each of equal importance, and each totally dependent on the other. You have already encountered the intimate link between 'Buddha' and 'Dharma' in the phrase 'He who sees me, sees the dharma. He who sees the dharma, sees me.' You have also seen that at the same time as the dharma being true, regardless of whether or not there was a Buddha, the appearance of the Buddha has made the Dharma accessible to others – so he is of great importance. The Sangha, or community of people following the teachings of the Buddha, is equally important.

When the Buddha died he left his teachings in the hands of the Sangha. There was no book of scriptures and no successor. Amongst his very last words the Buddha told the Sangha 'be a lamp unto yourselves'. Thus, not only were the Sangha to be the custodians of the teachings, they were also to work them out in their own ways. Today it is the Sangha that keeps alive the teachings and practices of Buddhism.

Going for Refuge

When the Buddha was alive, his followers saw him and his teachings as a 'refuge'. In this case, the word 'refuge' has many meanings relating to the idea of something you can trust, somewhere where you can be safe, somewhere you can grow and develop, and somewhere you can get support. Buddhists thought of the world as full of the perils of ignorance, attachment and suffering, and Buddhism was a refuge from all this. As Buddhism grew, the community of followers also became a refuge. Many traditions of Buddhism see the Three Jewels as refuges and will chant them in Pali:

Buddham saranam gacchami	(I go the Buddha for refuge)
Dhammam saranam gacchami	(I go to the Dharma for refuge)
Sangham saranam gacchami	(I go to the Sangha for refuge)

This chanting is called 'Going for Refuge', and is an important part of Buddhist ritual. The formula above is chanted three times, so that each refuge is brought fully to mind. In chanting the formula Buddhists orientate themselves away from wordly things like money, ambition and romance, and toward the three jewels.

Sile, a Buddhist from Cardiff, spoke about the importance of going for refuge in her own life. Recently her family dog, Connor, had to be put down and she and her daughter Jacqui took him to the vet's. Although they realised it was the compassionate thing to do, they still felt the imminent loss of this ailing and good-natured family friend very deeply. Sile's daughter, though not a Buddhist herself, understood the Buddhist belief that this life is not the only life, even for animals, and they decided that it would be fitting to have a quiet moment to reflect on this just before the vet gave the injection.

Sile went for refuge by reciting the Pali formula three times. She explained that of course they were still upset, but that going for refuge helped them to cope with the transition. It helped them to focus less on their own grief, and more on Connor and his passing to a new existence.

'Buddhism', she said, 'teaches that parting from those we love is inevitable and that sorrow and suffering are a part of life. But also that ultimately, there is a way out of suffering, with the help of the Buddha, the Dharma and the Sangha, and that can be a great comfort in difficult times.'

During the time of the Buddha, the followers who had taken refuge in him and the teachings were known as Bhikkhus (P) (S. Bhikshus) which means 'those who share'. The Bhikkhus lived a wandering life, practising meditation, teaching the dharma, living outside and eating only what was given to them. The Buddha sent them out with the words:

'Go monks and travel for the welfare and happiness of the people, out of compassion for the world. Teach the Dharma.' Vinaya 1:21

Bhikkhus did not perform the extreme austerities such as those performed by the Buddha during the six years after his renunciation, because the Buddha had declared such practices as inconsistent with the middle way, and unhelpful on the quest for enlightenment. However, they did give up their lives of worldly affairs, since this was seen as helpful to the aim of overcoming attachments. The Sangha made everybody equal.

During the rainy season, the Bhikkhus would come together take a break from wandering and stay in a vihara or monastery. This happened during the lifetime of the Buddha as well as after it. In the modern world, most monks live permanently in viharas and few are homeless wanderers.

After the death of the Buddha the Bhikkhus would recite the teachings, and give accounts of whether they had been able to keep the precepts (rules). This recitation ensured that the teachings of the Buddha were kept alive, and everybody agreed on what they were. Of course, as time went by people took different views on the nature of some of the teachings, but this was more to do with the fact that the Sangha was a democratic community than with the failure of oral tradition (recitation) to preserve teachings.

The Bhikkhu Sangha was entirely reliant for its support on the lay (not ordained) followers of the Buddha. Many lay followers were very generous during the lifetime of the Buddha, For instance, a wealthy merchant purchased a grove from a Prince called Jeta with enough gold pieces to entirely cover its ground, which he then donated to the Sangha. Even today

Seminar topic

Why is the act of teaching regarded as compassionate in Buddhism?

Bhikkhus are reliant on dana ('giving') from lay people for the upkeep of their viharas and for their food. Bhikkhus can eat no food unless it has been given to them. The act of giving has benefits for the giver as well as the receiver. In giving, a lay person gains 'merit' or puñña/punya. This could be described as positive karma.

If someone is committed to the path of enlightenment, and has made many sacrifices in the attempt to attain it, they are greatly respected. Their attainments are seen as benefiting the whole community because they are able to teach others the way out of suffering, so lay people are only too pleased to be of any assistance to their quest.

The Precepts

The Sangha (both lay and monk) commit themselves to the five precepts. Although precept literally means 'rule' these are not binding commandments, but rather goals towards which the Buddhist orientates him/herself.

I undertake to abstain from harming

This is understood in a very wide sense - killing or hurting, not only physically but also mentally and emotionally.

I undertake to abstain from taking anything that is not given

This does not only mean not stealing, but is a generous attitude towards others (for example, wanting them to do well) and not wasting their time and energy.

I undertake to abstain from misuse of the senses

This does not only mean not abusing sex (e.g. taking advantage or harming someone emotionally), it also means not desperately seeking pleasure the whole time.

I undertake to abstain from the misuse of speech

Not only is this about not lying, it is also about not gossiping or being argumentative. For Buddhists speech should be 'skilful'. In other words it should always help others on the path to enlightenment.

I undertake to abstain from taking any substance that clouds the mind

Buddhism is about being mindful - looking suffering and unsatisfactoriness straight in the eye, rather than trying to escape from it, which is the aim of those who abuse alcohol or take drugs.

Buddhism is a vast and diverse religion and Buddhists interpret these basic precepts in a variety of different ways. For instance, in many Buddhist countries, drinking alcohol in moderation is perfectly acceptable. For some Buddhists, the first precept means that vegetarianism is the only option, for others the precept refers to interaction only with humans. For some Buddhists the first precept makes it impossible to consider abortion or euthanasia. For other Buddhists compassion could in some circumstances result in abortion or euthanasia being acceptable.

Theravada monks on an alms round. The Sangha relies on the food donated to it by the lay people. Members of the monastic Sangha are not allowed to cook or grow their own food. This means that there can only be a monastic Sangha where the lay people want one. This helps to keep the Sangha relevant to the needs of the lay people.

The Monastic Precepts

In addition to the Five Precepts that are followed by both lay people and monks, there are five other precepts that are followed only by monks. These are:

To abstain from eating after midday

To abstain from dancing or singing

To abstain from using perfume or garlands

To abstain from sleeping on comfortable beds

To abstain from handling money

Task

Writing task	Explain the meaning of the monastic precepts.

In addition to the ten monastic precepts, there are other rules that monks try to live up to. There are 227 of them, and they are to be found in the Vinaya Pitaka (or the set of scriptures that contain the rules of conduct for monks and nuns). Some of these rules were established during the time of the Buddha, but the Vinaya Pitaka also contains material that was agreed on by the Sangha after the death of the Buddha.

The 227 rules are called the Patimokka, and even today the Theravada Sangha comes together regularly on days known as Uposatha days, to recite the Patimokka.

In Theravada Buddhism the idea of a monastic life is central. In countries such as Sri Lanka, Myanmar and Thailand, and indeed in Western Theravada Monasteries such as Amaravati in Hertfordshire, it is customary for life to begin very early in the morning (even before 3am!) for meditation and puja (ritual devotion). Then the monks will go out to receive food from lay people. This is sometimes described as begging, but that can be misleading. The monks do not beg anyone to give them food. They just receive whatever is offered. After eating the food before midday, they will do any work necessary for the upkeep of the vihara and of both the monastic and lay community (for instance, many viharas have schools or clinics or hospitals attached to them.)

The Amaravati Monastery, Hertfordshire.

Theravada Bhikkhus have no possessions of their own, though they are allowed to use robes (usually saffron yellow in colour because that is the cheapest dye), a bowl in which to receive offered food, a razor, a water strainer and a needle with which to darn their robes.

Chapter 8

Initiation

In the Theravada tradition distinctions are made within the monastic Sangha. Someone who has made a partial commitment is described as an anagarika ('homeless'). Anagarikas wear white robes and follow many of the Patimokka rules. They are, however, able to handle money, so are very useful to viharas. Many monks begin their careers as anagarikas, but if they want to fully commit themselves to the Sangha they become novices.

To become a novice a person must have no partner or debts (i.e. no worldly commitments). Often young boys will join the Sangha. It is thought to result in good karma to spend even a short time as a novice. There is no shame in leaving the Sangha, so short periods of time have become a feature of the lives of men in many Theravada communities. The novice has his head shaved, often by his parents, with whom he will remain in touch, and he will be given his robe. He then takes the Ten Precepts. 'Taking' the precepts is a bit like 'going' for refuge. It means reciting them as a statement of orientation and aspiration. After two years a novice may become a Bhikkhu. Some Bhikkhus become Theras or 'Elders' and some Theras become Mahatheras (great elders). Traditionally in Tibetan Buddhism, many boys take the opportunity to spend a period of time (perhaps a few years) following the religious life, and receive their education from senior monks or lamas.

In some forms of Chinese and Japanese Buddhism, people are not asked to renounce family life in order to become ordained members of the Sangha. Such people are usually referred to as Buddhist priests rather than monks. The philosophy behind this is that enlightenment is available to all people (see page 20) so therefore emphasis should not be put on monasticism. You can become enlightened whether you renounce or not. Priests could be understood to be much more relevant to lay people, because of the similarity between their lifestyles.

Women in Buddhism

Like almost every religion the world over, at different points in its history Buddhism could be considered to have valued men above women. The Buddha was very hesitant to allow women into the monastic Sangha of his time, but he was persuaded by Ananda, one of his disciples, to ordain his step-mother and five hundred other women in to the Bhikkhuni (female version of Bhikkhu) order. After that, however, many women became Bhikkhunis, and one of the earliest pieces of literature to have been written by women, the Therigata (verses of the sisters) was compiled. This scripture speaks of the liberation that women found in joining the Sangha, which was a regulated community in which they were free from the abuse and exploitation of lay life.

Considering the general attitude to women at the time (i.e. that they were ritually impure inferior beings and unable to participate in religious rituals) the Buddha was ahead of his time, and his hesitation is perhaps understandable in its historical context. Bhikkhunis were bound by many more Patimokka rules than Bhikkhus, which reflects their status at the time. There was a fear that women could distract the men from their commitment to attaining enlightenment, and that situation needed to be avoided for everybody's sake.

Seminar topic

How valuable is the monastic Sangha to lay Buddhists?

The Bhikkhuni Order, founded by the Buddha, died out in Theravada countries. The reason for this was that five nuns were always required in order to ordain another. If there were not five nuns in a country the 'ordination line' was broken. By approximately 1,000 years after the Buddha, most Theravada ordination lines had been broken. It is now possible to become a female novice, but not a full Theravada Bhikkhuni. In Mahayana countries it is possible to become a nun. For instance, in Taiwan there are many more nuns than there are monks and their status is high. Man Yao, pictured on page 32 is a very senior nun, respected within her community and with many responsibilities.

There are many Zen Nuns, and they are considered as the equal of Zen monks. Why do you think this is?

The wider Sangha in Britain

It is easy to find out about Sanghas in Britain, because many of them have sites on the Internet. Taraloka is a women's retreat centre in North Wales belonging to the Friends of the Western Buddhist Order, a Buddhist tradition founded in 1967 by an Englishman. You can learn about their aims and activities at **http://www.taraloka.org.uk**

In Powys there is a centre for the practice of Samatha meditation. Visit it at **http://www.samatha.demon.co.uk**

Check out the Friends of the Western Buddhist Order Centre in Cardiff at **http://www.cardiffbuddhistcentre.com**

Alternatively you can search most of the centres in Britain, regardless of their type, from BuddhaNet:

http://www.buddhanet.net

Chapter 8

Tasks

Writing tasks	Explain why renunciation of worldly life might be considered helpful on the path to enlightenment
	Assess the view that monastic life is escapist as it does not engage with the real world.
	Explain the significance of the monastic precepts and the patimokka for monks and nuns.
	'The path to enlightenment is the path to freedom; there should be no need for rules and regulations.' Evaluate this view.
	Draft a set of rules and regulations for a new modern Sangha in Wales.

Glossary

anagarika	'homeless', those who have made a partial commitment to the monastic sangha and keep some of the patimokka rules.
Bhikkhu	Theravadin monks.
Bhikkuni	A Theravadin nun.
Buddham saranam gacchami	'To the Buddha I go for refuge'.
Dhammam saranam gacchami	'To the Dharma I go for refuge'.
lama	'Higher one', a teacher in the Tibetan tradition.
Patimokka	The set of 227 rules for monks and 311 for nuns.
precepts	Obligations that Buddhists undertake. There are five for lay people, and ten for monks and nuns.
Sangham saranam gacchami	'To the community I go for refuge'.
Thera	'elder', a senior member of a monastic sangha.
Therigata	Part of the Pali canon, containing stanzas written by nuns.
Triratna	The three jewels of Buddhism (Buddha, Dharma and Sangha).
vihara	Monastery (Theravada).
Vinaya	The portion of the Pali Canon that contains the code of discipline for the Sangha.

Meditation

Aim

After studying this chapter you should understand the nature and role of some different meditation forms, and you should be able to evaluate their relevance to life.

Meditation is one of the central practices of most forms of Buddhism. However, one important form of Buddhism does not use meditation to attain enlightenment. Japanese Pure Land Buddhists believe that if you meditate you run the risk of reinforcing your sense of self (and not undermining it, which is the purpose of meditation in other Buddhist traditions). You may end up thinking 'I've done a lot of meditation today, so I must be much nearer my goal of enlightenment.' You may even end up thinking 'I've done much more meditation than my fellow Buddhists – therefore I'm much better than them!' (Where has anatta gone??) As unenlightened human beings we can't help falling into such unwholesome ways of thinking.

Pure Land Buddhists say we should face up to the reality of our own inability to achieve enlightenment through our own efforts (this realisation is extremely difficult, because humans are fundamentally arrogant about their abilities!). We should rely totally on the merit and grace of Amitabha (Amida), a great bodhisattva who vowed to bring all beings to enlightenment. They see this reliance on another power as the full realisation of anatta.

However, although their arguments make sense from a Buddhist point of view, the followers of Pure Land Buddhism are in the minority. Most Buddhists advocate the practice of meditation. After all, it was through meditation that the Buddha attained enlightenment under the Bodhi tree some 2,500 years ago. The Buddha is seen as an example to others on the path and most Buddhists believe he (as well as other enlightened beings) should be imitated.

> **For reflection**
>
> *Can you see any sense in the Japanese Pure Land view of meditation?*

Meditation is difficult to explain to people who have not had some experience of it. On the face of it, it looks like an extremely boring activity to engage with. Buddhists are often described as 'navel-gazers' or 'escapist' because of this distinctive practice of meditation. Buddhists would want to describe all of these views as misunderstanding the purpose of the practice.

Meditation is not merely about stress-busting, though that is certainly an important side-effect of the practice. It is about seeing into the true nature of things and developing, though rigorous training, the virtue of mindfulness. In our normal daily lives we are driven this way and that, by the routines that we are too weak to break with, by our goals and desires and by our greed and hatred. (Don't forget that in Buddhism there is nothing wrong with goals and desires, unless they become selfish and negative. The genuine desire for the happiness of others, for example, is a good desire and is central to Buddhism). Merv Fowler describes the mind as 'like some farmyard dog on a chain, which surges first this way then that, without ever making any real progression.'[7] We are not fully aware of our own motivations and intentions, unless we actually stop and take time to reflect on them.

Chapter 9

Seminar topic

Is meditation in Buddhism a substitute for prayer?

For Buddhists, the body is one skandha amongst the five, all of which are of equal importance (Buddhism is not a religion like Christianity or Hinduism that sees the soul as more important than the body). Meditation involves the body as well as the other skandhas.

The body is positioned so that the person is both relaxed and alert. Some Buddhists adopt the lotus position seen in statues of the Buddha, others sit astride cushions in a kneeling position, or cross-legged, or on a straight backed chair.

There are many different forms of meditation in the different traditions of Buddhism. In Tibet, for instance, there are different meditations on the enlightened beings. In some traditions of Buddhism, walking meditation is practised. Some traditions, such as Zen, emphasise the need to see all life as a meditation, even mundane daily chores.

We shall look briefly at three types here: **Samatha**, or calmness meditation **Vipassana**, or insight meditation which are both from the Theravada Tradition, and **Zazen**, or sitting meditation which is from Zen Buddhism – a form of Mahayana Buddhism.

Samatha

Samatha meditation begins with the breath. Being aware of one's breathing helps to heighten awareness that the body is a process, in which all the skandhas are in flux. Focusing on breathing also helps to train the mind to become detached from any distractions, and to master the ability not to be overcome by thoughts that arise, but to observe them arise and pass away.

Paul came to Buddhism because of his interest in martial arts, especially Kung Fu: 'Without the philosophical background of Buddhism, Kung Fu becomes just another sport. I particularly respect the teachings of the Vietnamese Monk, Thich Nhat Hanh, about mindfulness of breathing, the questioning of why we do things, and about being fully alive to the moment.'

For reflection

What does Paul mean by the 'mindfulness of breathing' and being 'fully alive to the moment'? Are the two connected? If so, how?

For reflection

How realistic is the metta bhavana? Could such practice be accurately described as escapist or 'navel gazing'? (Remember the close link in Buddhism between intention and action.)

Samatha also involves the metta bhavana, or the meditation on love, in which the person meditating cultivates loving feelings. These loving feelings are sometimes described as the brahmaviharas or 'godlike states' (godlike because they involve unconditional love - something that does not come naturally to humans). There are four of them. The first is metta, or loving-kindness, which the practitioner is asked to cultivate even for enemies. The second, karuna, is compassion for all the suffering experienced by others. The third is mudita, which is sympathetic joy. The celebration of the goodness or the achievement of others is very difficult, especially if one has not done so well oneself. The fourth, uppekkha, is equanimity, which means loving all beings equally (a very hard thing to do!)

Vipassana

This is a much more complicated system of meditation and involves what Damien Keown describes as 'the generation of penetrating and critical insight'.[8] The meditator tries to realise the truths of dukkha, anicca and anatta, though the observation of their own body, feelings, moods and thoughts. Feelings, moods and thoughts can be observed to arise and then to pass away – because just like the body, the mind is constantly in flux. In this way the meditator is trained not be driven by desire, hatred, greed, anger and so on. In recognising that both the body and all the other aspects of self (the skandhas) are in flux, the meditator realises that the idea of the ego or self is an illusion, and is thus liberated from thinking in terms of 'me' and 'mine'.

Zazen

Zazen literally means sitting-meditation. Zen, the form of Buddhism that uses Zazen, is influenced by the Mahayana philosophy that nirvana and samsara are two sides of the same coin, or to put it another way, they are both in the here and now. If one perceives with the eye of wisdom, nirvana is in this very moment. In addition to this understanding of the presence of nirvana, Zen teaches that too much attention to teachings and scriptures can end up confusing the mind, rather than leading it to the clarity of enlightenment. This view comes from the idea that our words, concepts and habits of mind are 'unenlightened', and are therefore unlikely to help us to perceive the truth. They are in fact more likely to lull us into wrongly thinking that we know what truth, or enlightenment, is.

Zazen, therefore, does not ask the meditator to contemplate dukkha, anicca or anatta, or to analyse the nature of the changing skandhas. They simply sit, using intuition to attain the realisation that the truth of nirvana is here and now.

Western Buddhists meditate at the Tibetan Buddhist Centre in Lambeth, South London.

There is a traditional story in Zen that is used to illustrate this 'intuition':

The Buddha was always asked by his followers to answer questions about the nature of the universe, whether it was created and whether there was life after death (i.e. 'metaphysical speculation' see page 37). He never answered these questions directly, but on one particular occasion he simply picked a flower and held it up. His followers were understandably bemused and frustrated. But one Bhikkhu, Mahakashyapa, smiled. In that enigmatic and puzzling smile, say Zen Buddhists, was the beginning of Zen itself. If any attempt were made to explain what Mahakashyapa was smiling at, then that clear insight into the truth would be muddied and spoiled by our own unenlightened ideas. That smile was simply a moment of intuition.

Chapter 9

Zen is sometimes described as 'direct pointing to reality', so it might be helpful to describe Mahakashyapa's smile as a direct realisation of reality. This direct realisation lies outside of words, teachings, concepts, and is wholly intuitive, and it is exactly that realisation that Zazen practitioners attempt to attain in their simple practice of sitting.

For Zen Buddhists, meditation is not something that happens only when one is sitting in the meditation hall. Even everyday tasks can become meditations upon nirvana. Nirvana is in the here and now, if we could but see and experience it, so even the most mundane of chores becomes transformed into the blissful experience of enlightenment. It is for this reason that a popular image of Zen monks and nuns is that they live a very simple life, just chopping wood for the fire, or getting water from the well, or preparing the vegetables, or sweeping the courtyard. These humdrum activities are meditations; they are performed with mindful awareness that they are the very stuff of nirvana.

For reflection

'To say that truth lies outside of words and concepts makes no sense at all.' Do you agree? Why/why not?

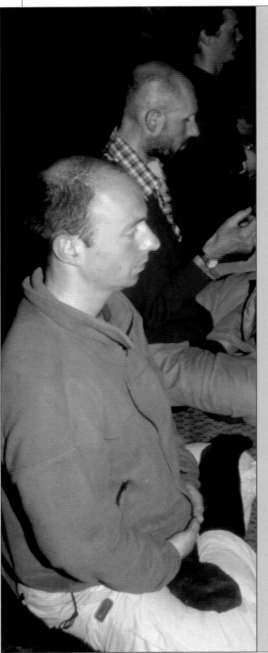

Surana is an Ordained member of the Western Buddhist Order. Here he explains what meditation means to him.

'When I first started meditating, in May 1986, I assumed that by the end of the summer I would have attained enlightenment. 15 years later I have revised my ambitions! While enlightenment remains the ultimate goal, the time scale has been amended.

In 1986 I was a fairly typical, confused, and somewhat unhappy 21-year-old. Initially my aspiration was in part informed by the desire to escape the pain and confusion. On the other hand there was within that young man I was, a desire to understand myself, to find meaning, contentment and happiness in life and ultimately develop a degree of wisdom, a genuine understanding of life. These are still motivating factors in my desire to meditate.

Over these years my understanding and practice of meditation has changed. I was not a 'natural' meditator. Although I had confidence in its efficacy I often struggled. I found it hard to meditate and sometimes got headaches and felt 'spaced-out'. But in addressing these difficulties, by finding more intelligent ways of meditating, I was without realising it addressing issues in my own mind. I didn't experience the bliss that I had anticipated but I was transforming my mind and my approach both to myself and to life.

Engaging in life was always a part of my motivation for meditating. I had something of a contempt for people who wanted to meditate and preciously sit aloof from the world. Equally I could see plenty of people rushing around 'doing good' but getting into thoroughly miserable states of mind. Meditation can and does to some extent help approach life in a balanced manner - being active yet composed and positive. Thankfully these days it's all a lot more straightforward and enjoyable. I meditate more or less everyday, getting up around 7 a.m. to meditate for the best part of an hour. While I don't get into higher states of consciousness I do enjoy it and find it nourishing.

It's not really easy to convey a subjective experience like meditation, because we all have different ways of articulating ourselves. Somehow by meditating I become a little bit more three dimensional and present. When I don't get a chance to meditate, or only for short periods, life becomes tighter and grey. Since parallel life experiments are impossible, I can never know what I would have been like had I not meditated. That enlightenment is apparently no closer than it was (3 summer months was a wee bit ambitious!!) does not concern me at all. I am simply grateful I have spent 15 years meditating . . . and who knows what will happen in the next 15 years !'

For reflection

Are you surprised that Surana says that he is not concerned at all by the fact he is no nearer enlightenment? If so why? If not, why not?

Surana uses some figurative language to speak about his experiences. For example he says that when he doesn't meditate, life becomes 'tighter and grey', and when he does meditate he feels he is more 'three dimensional and present'. What do you think he means by this?

Task

Writing tasks	Explain how Buddhists meditate.
	'Meditation is more likely to reinforce someone's sense of self than to undermine it'. Assess the validity of this view.

Seminar topic

Is Surana right to worry about people who rush around 'doing good' but getting into thoroughly miserable states of mind.'? Surely doing good is all that matters?

Chapter 9

Glossary

Brahmaviharas	God-like states. The four qualities that the Buddhist tries to develop through meditation, known as god-like because they involve unconditional love, which is very difficult for humans.
karuna	Compassion. One of the characteristics of Buddhas and Bodhisattvas, especially in the Mahayana tradition, and one of the four Brahmaviharas.
Mahakashyapa	One of the Buddha's principle disciples, who features in the traditional story of the founding of Zen Buddhism.
metta	Loving kindness. One of the four Brahmaviharas.
metta bhavana	A form of meditation that embraces all beings in loving-kindness
mudita	'sympathetic joy. One of the four Brahmaviharas
Pure Land Buddhism	A form of Mahayana Buddhism that believes enlightenment is only possible in the Pure Land of Amida Buddha, into which the adherent who despairs of attaining enlightenment by their own efforts is born.
samatha	Calmness meditation.
Thich Nhat Hanh	A Vietnamese Buddhist teacher whose teachings have become very famous in the West.
uppekkha	'equanimity'. One of the four Brahmaviharas.
Vipassana	'Insight meditation', insight into the lakshanas.
Zazen	'Sitting'. A form of meditation practised by the Soto Zen school.

Puja

Aim

After studying this chapter you should be aware of the form and symbolism of different types of puja in different Buddhist traditions. You should also have reflected on the nature of worship in the Buddhist context.

It is sometimes easy to forget that as well as all the rather intellectual and philosophical concepts and the austere practice of meditation, Buddhism is also about daily rituals and annual festivals that help to remind Buddhists of their aims, and of their relationship to Buddha, Dharma and Sangha.

One of the most striking features of Buddhism is the way its practices vary from country to country and from tradition to tradition. Most religions - let's consider Islam as an example - have a core set of practices that anyone who belongs to that religion will know about. Muslims all over the world will observe the obligation to pray five times a day facing the Ka'ba in Makkah. Whether in Britain, Indonesia or Saudi Arabia they will spend the month of Ramadan fasting and contemplating the Qur'an; they will celebrate the festivals of Eid al-Fitr and Eid-ul Adha, and they will greet each other with 'Al-salam alaykum'. Of course, there will be regional differences in the way these obligations are observed.

Buddhism is different. Traditions arose and developed in different ways after the Buddha's death. The Buddha gave the Sangha freedom when he appointed no successor to follow him, and Buddhism just developed in its own way. Because the Buddha always told his followers to 'test the teachings' and not to accept things merely on his authority (or anyone else's authority), many Buddhists would argue that they are free to do the things that they feel will help them best to follow the path, and to deepen their understanding of the qualities of enlightenment. At any rate, it could be argued that because Buddhism is a set of teachings for a purpose rather than a revelation of Absolute Truth, it can much more easily be changed and adapted to suit people of different ages, and people of different cultures.

> **Seminar topic**
>
> *Do you find it strange that not all Buddhists follow the same rituals or festivals? Why/why not.*
>
> *Is Buddhism really a 'whatever's best for you' religion?*

> *A shrine with a statue of the Buddha with his hands in the mudra of meditation.*
>
> *Do you think the use of such shrines reflects the desire for something aesthetically pleasing? Does this fit in with the Buddhist ideas? How do Buddhist use and think about shrines?*

Chapter 10

Puja

Most Buddhists, regardless of the tradition they belong to, regularly perform puja. Puja is a word that is also used in a Hindu context. Literally, it means 'worship', but it is very important to be completely clear about what this means. Because in the West the word 'worship' seems to imply the idea of an omnipotent creator God, some Buddhists feel that it is not an appropriate word to use in the case of Buddhism. After all, the Buddha is definitely not a God (see page 5), and generally speaking Buddhists do not believe in an omnipotent God who created the universe. Such Buddhists may prefer a word like 'veneration', which suggests respect rather than worship. However, technically, worship only means an activity or attitude directed towards something that you consider to be worthy, to have worth. Buddhists certainly believe the Buddha (and the Dharma and the Sangha for that matter) to be worthy – so perhaps worship is not such an odd word to use.

Seminar topic

Would you describe going for refuge in the three jewels as 'worship'?

Merit

All actions have consequences. Buddhists believe that by performing certain actions, with the right intentions, it is possible to purify your karma and to attain 'merit' (P. puñña/Skt. Punya). Such merit can help the individual on the path towards enlightenment, but it can also be shared with others. If you think about it, it would be rather selfish to do good only for the sake of one's own enlightenment. It is far more Buddhist to do good to help others. Therefore, part of puja involves willing the good that has been done in performing the puja to be passed to others to increase their store of merit. Performing puja is only one way of attaining merit that can be transferred to others. There are many others; for example, giving (dana) food or donations to the Sangha.

Peter Harvey, who is a British Theravada Buddhist, wrote in the front of his book on Buddhism:

'May any auspicious purifying power (puñña) generated by writing this work be for the benefit of my parents, wife and daughter, all who read this book, and all beings.'[9]

The structure of this dedication is very Buddhist. Remember the metta bhavana? This is the meditation that considers first the well being of oneself and those closest; then it moves out in concentric circles towards people with whom one has less close relationships. Harvey considers those closest to him first, namely, his immediate family. It is easiest to wish to benefit these people. What follows is more challenging. He wishes those who read the book to benefit. Don't forget, he is not saying he wishes them to benefit from reading the book, but that he wishes them to benefit from the puñña generated by him in writing the book. He intends this puñña to be for others. (Intention is all-important in Buddhism). He does not know everybody who will read his book. Perhaps he feels some kind of relationship or connection with them, but he is still wishing to benefit people he does not know. Then finally, he dedicates the puñña to all beings - people who are interested in Buddhism, but haven't read his book; people who are not interested in Buddhism; people who belong to other religions; good people, bad people; dead relatives and even non-human 'beings' (don't forget the human realm is one realm amongst many in Buddhism).

This is a typical Buddhist action. Whenever any good work is done, whether good deeds, works of scholarship or creativity, meditation, chanting, or puja, the person who has done it will state their determination for the merit attained to be transferred to someone other than themselves, and often to all beings.

For reflection

Does the idea of transfer of merit make any sense? (clue: think about the bodhisattva)

Puja rituals

Buddhists perform puja in the home or in the Temple. It involves making symbolic offerings to statues (or sometimes pictures) of the Buddha or other enlightened beings. Water for washing and water for drinking are offered, as water sustains life. Flowers, incense, light, food and perfume representing the five senses are also offered. It also involves bowing, sometimes with palms pressed together, or even fully prostrating in front of the image. To non-Buddhists this might look very much like the worship that would be offered to a god. However, these gestures of respect are part of the culture of the countries in which Buddhism is most popular. The Japanese, for instance, bow to each other all the time. This is not worship, but a show of respect for the other person. In bowing to a statue of the Buddha, Buddhists are not saying the Buddha is a god, just that what the statue stands for is worthy of respect.

The puja is likely to involve 'going for refuge' and the 'taking of the precepts'. This means those present will say or chant the refuges and precepts in Pali or Sanskrit, or Japanese or Tibetan, or even in English or Welsh, depending on the setting and the type of Buddhism being practiced. In Mahayana Buddhism there may be other ritual activities such as the chanting of sutras, the use of music, especially drums, gongs, bells and trumpets, the making of mudras (symbolic hand gestures), the contemplation of mandalas (symbolic images of enlightenment used in meditation) and the chanting of mantras.

In most forms of Buddhism, worshippers will also formally state their intention that any merit gained from their act of worship will be used for the benefit of others.

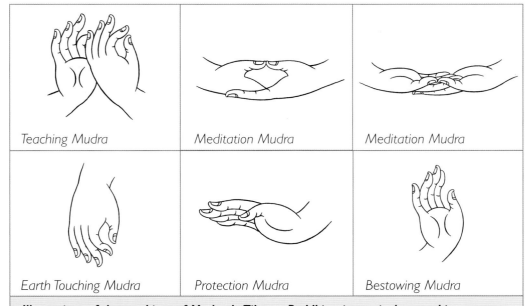

| Teaching Mudra | Meditation Mudra | Meditation Mudra |
| Earth Touching Mudra | Protection Mudra | Bestowing Mudra |

Illustrations of the teachings of Mudra. In Tibetan Buddhism in particular, worshippers themselves will make the mudras with their own hands, as the way of manifesting (bringing into being) the attributes that the mudras stand for.

Seminar topic

How can making hand movements be meaningful?

This mandala was made by five Tibetan monks who visited the Welsh village of Llandysul, shortly after the terroist attacks on America on September 11th 2001. It took the monks two weeks to make it out of coloured sand. The merit from making it was dedicated to the promotion of peace and compassion in the world. After visits from farmers and other residents of Llandysul, the mandala was washed away in a nearby stream. Part of the meaning of this ceremony is to remind those who participate of the insubstantiality and impermanence of all things.

What do the statues stand for?

The identity of a statue on the shrine depends largely on the type of Buddhism being practiced. Theravada Buddhist Temples and shrines have statues of the historical Buddha. In this case the statue represents the historical person who is worthy of respect because of what he achieved. He is contemplated upon because he is an inspiration and example to all people on the path to enlightenment.

In Mahayana Buddhism, statues may be of the historical Buddha, but they may also represent other enlightened beings; for instance, in Japan it is much more common to see Temples dedicated to Amida (Amitabha) than to the historical Buddha. Other enlightened beings commonly found include Manjusri, Avalokitesvara, or the five dhyani Buddhas (see page 21). These images are full of symbolism. They do not represent historical persons, rather aspects of enlightenment, or the qualities of enlightened beings that the Buddhist tries to imitate. For example, Manjusri's flaming sword that cuts through the darkness of ignorance represents the wisdom of seeing reality as it really is. When Mahayana Buddhists perform puja in front of a statue of Manjusri, they are showing their respect for the quality of wisdom, and their determination to develop it within themselves. The hands of any statue will be held in mudra.

Circumambulation of stupas

Some scholars argue that the Buddhist urge to show through ritual actions their respect for all that the Buddha stands for, comes from the practice in early Buddhism of visiting and circumambulating (ritually walking around) stupas containing the relics of the Buddha. In Theravada countries the circumambulation of stupas remains an important feature of worship. There is a picture of a stupa on page 17 (the Sanchi Stupa).

Prayer flags and prayer wheels

A mantra is a phrase containing the name of an enlightened being, that worshippers repeat, and in doing so they manifest the qualities of that enlightened being. An important mantra is the mantra of Avalokitesvara 'Om mani padme hum'. As Avalokitesvara is the Bodhisattva of compassion, contemplating and chanting this mantra is thought to help the worshipper manifest compassion.

Om mani padme hum in Tibetan. This mantra means 'Hail to the Jewel in the Lotus', which is one of the names of the Bodhisattva of Compassion.

In Tibetan Buddhism this mantra is written on flags, sometimes called prayer flags (although mantras are not prayers in the Christian sense) and on pieces of paper that are put inside prayer wheels, which the worshipper turns. In turning the wheel, the mantra is symbolically 'said'– thus generating more compassion.

Seminar topic

How can simply speaking a phrase, or even symbolically speaking it such as in the case of turning a prayer wheel, have any effect on anything?

Prayer flags on a Tibetan mountainside.

These prayer wheels contain thousands of mantras written on small pieces of paper. As she spins the wheel, this woman is symbolically sending out the mantras.

Tasks

Writing tasks	Explain some of the ways in which Buddhists worship. 'The Buddha is not a god, so Buddhists do not worship him'. Evalaute the validity of this view.
Presentation task	Produce a poster display that clearly illustrates the differences in the ways in which Buddhists worship.
Role Play	Role play a discussion between a Theravada Buddhist and a Tibetan Buddhist about what their worship means to them.

Glossary

mandala	A diagram used in mediation that depicts enlightenment. Often beautiful mandalas are constructed using coloured powder and chalks and then destroyed after a few days, as a reminder of impermanence.
mantra	Literally 'tool of the mind', a phrase containing the name of an enlightened being, which is repeated in order to manifest the qualities of that enlightened being.
mudra	Hand gestures with particular meanings. Statues of enlightened beings always have mudras, so that they can be identified and associated with a specific Buddhist idea. Mudras are often used in worship, especially in Tibetan Buddhism.
om mani padme hum	'Hail to the Jewel in the Lotus', the mantra of the bodhisattva of compassion, Avalokitesvara.
prayer flags	Flags with mantras written on them.
prayer wheels	Wheels containing mantras, which can be spun in order to symbolically 'say' the mantra many times.

Material for the Synoptic Unit (A2)

Throughout your study of Buddhism your teacher will have been alerting you to the information that you should bear in mind for the Synoptic Module that will be assessed at the end of your study of A2.

The assessment for the Synoptic module requires you to write an essay under controlled conditions on a specified aspect of either Religious Authority, or Religious Experience, or Life, Death and Life after Death. This essay should draw on at least two areas of study, because you are required to be able to sustain a critical line of argument, which may involve comparing and contrasting different areas of study.

As well as having the required knowledge and understanding of one of the three areas identified for synoptic assessment, you will need to demonstrate some critical reflection and the ability to sustain a line of argument.

Religious Authority

The question of authority is a very interesting one in Buddhism. The historical Buddha has authority as a human example of what it is possible to achieve. He also has authority as a teacher, who made recommendations to his followers for ways in which they could overcome craving and ignorance and achieve enlightenment. However, he did not issue commandments, and what he taught was not revelation in the Jewish, Christian or Islamic sense. Other sources of authority, arguably of equal value, are the Dharma and the Sangha.

The scriptures are also crucial, but it is important to remember that different types of Buddhists refer to different scriptures. There is no Buddhist 'Bible'!

An important source of authority in Buddhism is the individual. The Buddha told his followers not to simply accept anything he said, but to test out his recommendations and to see if they worked. Therefore, Buddhism is a personal quest in which the individual works out her own way to enlightenment.

Buddhism is of course institutionalised in many countries, and there are many high-ranking Buddhists who have authority in their particular kind of Buddhism. One example of such a person is the Dalai Lama.

Religious Experience

Buddhism is a religion that emphasises religious experience a great deal. The whole of the dharma was based on the religious experiences of one person, the Buddha. It is important to have reflected on the experiences that he is said to have had, and to try to imagine what it must have been like - to experience, for instance, the despair after seeing the Four Sights and the determination to find a way out of suffering for all beings. Most Buddhists would testify to having had religious experiences themselves. For example the accounts of Surana, Catherine, and Man Yao explain what it feels like to meditate, to come to a realisation of what is important in life, or to relate the practices of Buddhism to the individual's own life. These are all religious experiences.

Ideas of Life, Death and Life after Death

Buddhism has very clear ideas about the nature of life, death and life after death. The Buddhist analysis of the individual (explained on page 29) as being made up of five skandhas constantly in flux, provides the background to ideas about rebirth, becoming, karma and anatta or no-fixed-self. On the question of whether there is life after death, Buddhism usually steers a middle way between eternalism and nihilism.

Also important in this topic is the idea that human life is not the only kind of 'life'. There are other realms, with other kinds of suffering beings in them.

For further information and resources on religious experience contact the Religious Experience Research Centre, University of Wales Lampeter, Ceredigion, SA 48 7ED

ahardytrust@lamp.ac.uk   www.alisterhardytrust.org .

References

[1] Pye, Michael, *The Buddha*, London, Duckworth, 1979 p10

[2] Cush, Denise, *Buddhism (A Student's Approach to World Religions)*, London, Hodder and Stoughton, 1993, p45

[3] Rahula, Walpola, *What the Buddha Taught*, Oxford, Oneworld 1997

[4] Snelling, John, *The Buddhist Handbook: A complete guide to Buddhist teaching and practice*, London, Century, 1987

[5] Fowler, Merv, *Buddhism, Beliefs and Practices*, Brighton, Sussex Academic Press, 1999, pp50-51

[6] Gethin, Rupert, *The Foundations of Buddhism*, Oxford, Oxford University Press, 1998, p59

[7] Fowler, Merv, *Buddhism, Beliefs and Practices*, Brighton, Sussex Academic Press, 1999, p 73

[8] Keown, Damien, *A Very Short Introduction to Buddhism*, OUP, 1996, p92

[9] Harvey, Peter, *Introduction to Buddhism: Teachings, History and Practices*, CUP, 1990

Bibliography

Some recommended reading additional to books cited in the text.
Of these, especially useful are *Cush, Fowler* and *Gethin*

Clarke, Steve & Thompson Mel, *Buddhism: A New Approach*, London, Hodder & Stoughton, 1996 (this is designed for KS4 but is useful for AS)

Erricker, Clive, *Teach Yourself Buddhism*, London, Hodder& Stoughton, 2003

Harris, Elizabeth, *What Buddhists Believe*, Oxford, Oneworld, 1998

Harvey, Peter (ed) *Buddhism*, London, Continuum, 2001

Stokes, Gillian, *Buddha A beginner's Guide*, London Hodder & Stoughton, 2001

Skilton, Andrew, *A Concise History of Buddhism*, Birmingham, Windhorse, 1997

Thompson, Mel, *101 Key Ideas: Buddhism*, London, Hodder & Stoughton, 2000